SpringerBriefs in Education

SpringerBriefs in Citizenship Education for the 21st Century

Series Editor

Kerry J Kennedy, Curriculum and Instruction, The Education University of Hong Kong, Hong Kong, Hong Kong

More information about this subseries at http://www.springer.com/series/16233

Andrew Peterson

Civility and Democratic Education

Springer

Andrew Peterson
Jubilee Centre for Character and Virtues
University of Birmingham
Birmingham, UK

ISSN 2211-1921   ISSN 2211-193X   (electronic)
SpringerBriefs in Education
ISSN 2524-8480   ISSN 2524-8499   (electronic)
SpringerBriefs in Citizenship Education for the 21st Century
ISBN 978-981-15-1013-7   ISBN 978-981-15-1014-4   (eBook)
https://doi.org/10.1007/978-981-15-1014-4

This Springer imprint is published by the registered company Springer Nature Singapore Pte Ltd.
The registered company address is: 152 Beach Road, #21-01/04 Gateway East, Singapore 189721, Singapore

Preface

This book is dedicated to my mother and late father, to whom I owe a debt of gratitude for cultivating my interest in the exchange of political ideas and viewpoints. For a variety of reasons, these formative exchanges were always informal and occurred on a regular basis in response to given events of the day. The lack of formality and structure meant that ideas and positions could be discussed, reflected on and explored in open conversation, always with the understanding that exchanging passionately held differences was a healthy part of family life.

Conversely, my experience of schooling—in particular at the secondary level—provided very little opportunity for engaging in political discussion. Attending a high school in a selective system of education in the late 1980s and early 1990s, politics and social issues were missing altogether from our curriculum and lessons, and any attempt to even discuss politics in the classrooms was, with very few exceptions, met with disdain from teachers. Broadly speaking, little respect, let alone civility, existed between teachers and pupils and so it is perhaps no wonder that the school lacked a sense of community and little mutuality existed between pupils and the school (or, at least, that was my perception). Visiting a range of schools over the last 15 and more years to learn about their approaches to civic and character education has taught me that things can be, and often are, different to those conditions I encountered at school. Many schools I have had the honour of visiting are places where political issues and controversies can be discussed and reflected upon. Moreover, they are organisations in which a culture of civility has been cultivated between staff and pupils, as well as between pupils themselves.

I have a number of people to thank, all of whom have contributed to my writing of this book in various ways. First and foremost, I thank my family—Jessica, Oliver and George—for their love, support and humour. Second, I thank all of my colleagues at the Jubilee Centre for Character and Virtues for welcoming me into a vibrant, rigorous and collegial academic community. Third, I thank Alison Body, Laura D'Olimpio, Ralph Leighton and Lucas Walsh for their comments on various parts of the book as the manuscript was being developed. Their comments were extremely helpful in identifying areas in need of further clarification or analysis. Fourth, I thank the three anonymous reviewers who provided kind and perceptive comments on the manuscript. Fifth, I thank the series editor, Professor Kerry Kennedy, for his support for the book from proposal to publication. Sixth, and certainly not least, I also thank Lawrence Liu, Lay Peng Ang, Melody Zhang and Sophie Li at Springer for their support. Without each of the people mentioned here this book would not have been possible, though as ever any errors are mine alone.

In this book, I offer an exploration and examination of civility as an important part of democratic life and education. As I hope to show, it comes in the context of widespread concern about the levels of civility and incivility in Western democracies. As I also suggest, while civility cannot hope to cure all of the issues facing democracy today, without civility healthy democratic participation will not be possible.

Birmingham, UK   Andrew Peterson

Contents

1 The "Plight of Civility" Today 1
    Setting the Context: We Need to Talk About Civility 2
    Defining Civility 7
        Civility as a Civic Virtue 9
    The Structure of this Book 10
    References 11

2 Civil Conduct: Tolerance, Deliberation and the Possibility
of "Justified Incivility" 13
    Introduction 13
    Civility and Civil Conduct 14
        Civility and Tolerance 16
        Civility and Deliberation 21
    The Limits of Civility: Or When Is It Justified to Be Uncivil? 25
        The Excess and the Deficiency 28
        Justified Incivility 30
    Conclusion 32
    References 32

3 Civility and Mutual Fellow-Feeling 35
    Introduction 36
    Civic Friendship, Fellow-Feeling and Well-Wishing 37
        Civic Friendship 38
    Formative Processes 43
    Conclusion 47
    References 48

4 Educating Civility in Schools 51
    Introduction 51
    Situating Civility 53
    Experiencing Civility 57
    Enacting Civility 61

Conclusion 64
References... 65
5 **Moving Beyond the "Plight of Civility" and Future Research
   on Civility and Democratic Education** 69
   References... 73

Chapter 1
The "Plight of Civility" Today

Abstract This introductory chapter situates the focus of the book in the context of the (real or perceived) "plight of civility" affecting western democracies. Drawing mainly on the UK and the USA, examples of this plight are given. The chapter outlines the core approach to civility taken in the book, and does so in two ways. First, the distinction between *everyday* civility and *political* civility is drawn. Establishing the book's focus on the latter, it is argued that the concept of political civility comprises two components—civil conduct and mutual fellow-feeling. Drawing on Curzer's (Curzer, In: Civility in politics and education, Routledge, New York, 2012a; Curzer, Aristotle and the virtues. Oxford University Press, Oxford, 2012b) understanding of civility as an Aristotelian virtue, it is argued that civility can usefully be viewed as an intermediate mean between an excess (unfailing civility) and a deficiency (incivility). Some broad reasons are offered for conceiving civility as an important civic virtue and as a key marker of the health of democratic life. The chapter also sets out the structure and focus of the remainder of the book.

Keywords Civility · "Plight of civility" · Civil conduct · Fellow-feeling · Virtue

For a number of reasons, civility and incivility have come under much scrutiny in recent years across western democracies (which are my focus in this book[1]). Whether it is calls for greater civility in public life, the bemoaning of a lack of civility in political discourse or the assertion that everyday life has become increasing rude, there seems to be a general consensus that civility is both important and necessary for a healthy democracy and society. Yet, and as any academic discussion of civility usually starts, civility is not altogether easy to define. While it may be the case that, strictly speaking, "civility is a relative newcomer to the virtues"

---

[1] I am aware that other cultures and traditions have rich lines of thought about civility, but these are not the focus of this book.

A. Peterson, *Civility and Democratic Education*, SpringerBriefs in Education, https://doi.org/10.1007/978-981-15-1014-4_1

1

(Ward 2017, p. 119) it would be hard to accept that leading thinkers in the western canon were not aware of the importance within political communities of what today equates to civility. Jamieson et al. (2015) suggest that civility did not become a popular term until Erasmus' *De Civilitate Morum Puerilium* in the sixteenth century, while others have claimed that it has close similarities with ancient virtues such as self-control and moderation (Fiala 2013; Barrett 1991; Jamieson et al. 2015). Furthermore, while for some civility is a rather weak virtue lacking the depth and humanity of other virtues while also conjuring up historical notions of etiquette associated with the ruling classes, for others civility is a key marker of a healthy democracy. Not unconnected, critics have pointed out that in practice civility has been frequently used by those with power to constrain and dominate the interests and behaviours of those they wish to subjugate.

My interest in this book is in civility as a civic virtue for democratic life and participation. From here on in, and unless otherwise stated, I use the term "civility" to refer more specifically to what I define later in this introduction as *political* civility. My purpose is to examine the potential for, and of, a more positive reading of civility as a civic virtue vital for healthy, functioning democracies. Broadly speaking, my argument is that where democratic political communities exhibit high levels of civility, these communities will be more cohesive and stable. Where incivility is rife, those communities will more likely be divided and unstable. From the outset, it should be clear that this is not to suggest that certain forms of "incivility" are not acceptable. I will argue, instead, that certain actions that may be deemed as "uncivil" may well be valid and much needed responses to protect the interests of those marginalised arbitrarily by dominant powers; they are, I shall suggest, instances of "justified incivility". The reading of civility I propose rests on understanding civility in political life as a democratic virtue that is supported by feelings of mutual fellow-feeling and concern within political communities. This reading also offers particular challenges and opportunities for democratic education, and these also fall within the remit of this book (in particular in Chap. 4).

The remainder of this introduction comprises three sections. The first sets the context for this book, and provides an overview of the recent, and fairly widespread, concerns that have arisen about civility's decline in western democracies, particularly in the UK and the USA. The second section introduces the definition of civility pursued in the book. This definitional work starts by distinguishing between everyday and political civility. Focusing on the latter, and drawing on key ideas in the existing literature, political civility is defined as a democratic virtue and as comprising two core components: civil conduct and mutual fellow-feeling. The brief third section sets out the structure and focus of the remainder of the book.

Setting the Context: We Need to Talk About Civility

While I wish to take a positive stance regarding the value of civility for contemporary, western democracies and, by extension, for democratic education, it is necessary to start the analysis with a recognition that many discussions of civility in political life start from the premise that civility has declined and that incivility has increased. Indeed, for a number of years now concerns have been rife that public discourse in western democratic societies has become increasingly *uncivil*. A simple internet search of incivility in politics identifies numerous think pieces, research studies and other articles that identify the incivility problem. While assertions that civility is in decline cannot be fully isolated from wider theses on the decline of public life more generally (as expressed in amongst others in Putnam's (2000) *Bowling Alone*, Sennett's (2003) *The Fall of Public Man* and Marquand's (2004) *Decline of the Public*), with seeming regularity public officials, commentators and organisations bemoan a decline in *civility* and a rise in *incivility*, evidenced they suggest by polarised political and social divisions, argumentation drawn from emotional rather than rational bases, and a tendency for discourse to collapse into ad hominem attacks. There has been and is, according to some, a "civility crisis" (Carter 1998; Bejan 2017; Boatright et al. 2019). The concern, considered in more detail below, is that citizens are becoming more entrenched in their views, refusing to engage critically with alternative positions, and are treating those who think and feel differently about important matters as not just holding disagreeable views, but as being disagreeable, morally inferior and perhaps even evil people.

This "uncivil war", so the thesis goes, has fundamentally changed the nature of political debate (for example, in the UK see Griffith et al. 2011; Phillips and Stuart 2019; in Australia see Kurti 2018; in Germany see Gümplová 2016; in the USA see Carter 1998; American Psychological Association 2018). But what are the precise features of public discourse that are viewed as signifying the decline in civility? A general list of these concerns about civility in political discourse would include the following concerns:

- That political ideas and debates are polarised, with different actors refusing to concede and compromise, frequently "talking past" each other;
- That political discourse can descend into personal, ad hominem attacks where engagement with ideas and standpoints is side-stepped in favour of discrediting the character and motivations of those holding different positions;
- That limited forms of civility (such as those that view civility as akin to manners) can breed superficial harmony, hiding deeper motives, disagreements and prejudices;
- That claims to "civility" and accusations of "incivility" can reinforce the values and power of dominant groups, often informed and shaped by class, ethnic and colonial histories;[2]
- That new technologies, including digital and social media, are fostering new arenas for incivility, particularly where interlocutors can hide behind anonymous profiles[3] and where social media platforms are used to politically vilify and ridicule others;

---

[2] See Nehring (2011) for an overview.

[3] In a recent study, Santana (2014, p. 27) found that "anonymous commenters wrote 65 percent of the uncivil comments while non-anonymous commenters did so in 35 percent of the comments...

– That political discussions, aided by new ways that political information, ideas and views are shared and received, often occur in an echo chamber within which citizens surround themselves with ideas and perspectives that support their already held positions, refusing to acknowledge and engage with contrary positions.

Often, though not always, present in accounts of civility's decline is the identification of what and whom are to blame. Here, various reasons abound.[4] Some identify a wider decline in civic virtue and commitment to public life, understanding the rise in incivility to be one part of this more general trend. Others point to the ways in which market and consumerist discourses, particularly those associated with various forms of neoliberalism, have impacted negatively on various social associations through which civility can be fostered and exhibited. Still others identify associated and destructive trends towards individualisation that also serve to rupture the bonds between citizens. In their analysis, Phillips and Stuart (2019) identify a movement away from a politics of the centre ground and pragmatism towards a politics of polarisation and ideology. Commentators from different parts of the political spectrum point the finger of blame at each other, whether it be social liberals critical of social conservatives or vice versa. Some even blame themselves. Following the admission that Facebook sold political advertising space to fake accounts designed to create divisions during the 2016 US elections,[5] Mark Zuckerberg issued an apology in which he stated "for those I hurt this year, I ask forgiveness and I will try to be better. For the ways my work was used to divide people rather than bring us together, I ask forgiveness and I will work to do better".[6]

Amidst this persistent worrying about civility's decline, we should also not lose sight of the fact that calls for greater civility may be mere words, often masking uncivil actions and abuses of power to silence or demonise others. In Chap. 1, I examine more challenging instances of such cases, but for now consider the following two examples. In his installation address as Speaker of the US House of Representatives in 1995, Newt Gingrich spoke boldly about cooperative politics:

> I want us to dedicate ourselves to reach out in a genuinely nonpartisan way to be honest with each other. I promise each of you that without regard to party my door is going to be open. I will listen to each of you. I will try to work with each of you. I will put in long hours, and I will guarantee that I will listen to you first. I will let you get it all out before I give you my version, because you have been patient with me today, and you have given me a chance to set the stage… All I can do is pledge to you that, if each of us will reach out prayerfully and try to genuinely understand each other, if we will recognize that in this building we

---

Of the… civil comments… non-anonymous commenters weighed in with 25.3 percent of the civil comments while anonymous comments (sic) did so with 74.7 percent of the comments".

[4] See Cohen (2018).

[5] https://www.independent.co.uk/life-style/gadgets-and-tech/news/facebook-russia-ads-us-election-political-adverts-trump-putin-fake-news-a7933461.html

[6] https://www.independent.co.uk/life-style/gadgets-and-tech/news/facebook-mark-zuckerberg-donald-trump-election-russia-political-ads-fake-news-a7978151.html

symbolize America, and that we have an obligation to talk with each other, then I think a year from now we can look on the 104th Congress as a truly amazing institution without regard to party, without regard to ideology.

Gingrich has subsequently been roundly blamed for playing a leading role in the decline in civility in US politics, being accused of fostering a culture of unhealthy partisanship and personal attacks on political adversaries[7] (BBC 2019). More recently, days before leaving office, UK Prime Minister Teresa May stated her concern about the "state of politics" in the UK echoing Gingrich's sentiments of cooperation and compromise, while warning that:

> The alternative is a politics of winners and losers, of absolutes and of perpetual strife—and that threatens us all. Today an inability to combine principles with pragmatism and make a compromise when required seems to have driven our whole political discourse down the wrong path. It has led to what is in effect a form of "absolutism"—one which believes that if you simply assert your view loud enough and long enough you will get your way in the end. Or that mobilising your own faction is more important than bringing others with you. This is coarsening our public debate. Some are losing the ability to disagree without demeaning the views of others. Online, technology allows people to express their anger and anxiety without filter or accountability. Aggressive assertions are made without regard to the facts or the complexities of an issue, in an environment where the most extreme views tend to be the most noticed.[8]

Within minutes, May was accused of hypocrisy and of having not practiced what she was now preaching throughout her time in office—including by Baroness Warsi, former co-chair of the Conservative Party.[9]

Taken together, the various concerns briefly outlined here also say something about the wider public culture in which, and through which, civility and incivility operate. Journalist Michael Goldfarb describes the decline in civility thesis and the general culture of incivility in the following terms:

> Nothing comes out of nothing. America didn't just wake up one day with a President who talks like he is in a locker room and politicians who can't speak politely to one another. The long incivil war in American political life has been going on for at least a quarter of a century. (BBC 2019)

As Goldfarb's reflection underscores, civility and incivility are not wholly characterised by particular individual acts. When we denounce a particular act in public life as being "uncivil" or celebrate another as being "civil" we are not just commenting on the specific act in isolation, but are saying something too about the wider context in which those acts occur. To press this point, when a politician resorts to lies and personal attacks on a member of another political party, their words are deemed uncivil not only because they insult the other person but also because they

---

[7] https://www.theatlantic.com/politics/archive/2016/07/newt-broke-politicsnow-he-wants-back-in/491390/; https://www.theatlantic.com/magazine/archive/2018/11/newt-gingrich-says-youre-welcome/570832/

[8] https://www.gov.uk/government/speeches/pm-speech-on-the-state-of-politics

[9] https://www.bbc.co.uk/news/uk-politics-49015559

impact negatively on the wider democratic culture and are suggestive that a negative form of discourse is—tacitly or otherwise—being accepted.

If the decline in civility thesis is indeed correct, then it is not hard to see why the tone and conduct of public discourse is viewed as being under threat. Yet, it is not clear precisely whether civility is on the decline as some would suggest and as some assume without really justifying their claim.[10] It is patently the case that, real or not, concerns about civility are not new (for a more detailed history of the concept, see Nehring 2011; Bejan 2017; Thomas 2018). Indeed, it would not be too melodramatic to posit that civility may be in a state of "perpetual crisis". Political life and discourse in the USA provides a case in point, with concerns regarding a decline in civility in public discourse a reasonably recurrent theme since the end of the Second World War (see, for example, Walzer 1974; Bloom 1987; Carter 1998). If we turn our attention to the UK, it could also be suggested that the plight of civility is not necessarily a recent phenomenon. It would be difficult to claim, for example, that recent political tensions over the UK's membership of the European Union were any less civil/more uncivil than tensions over the war in Iraq in the 2000s, the Poll Tax riots in 1990, the Miners' strike in the 1980s, the troubles in Northern Ireland, the anti-nuclear campaign and the (ongoing) fights for equal rights for women and ethnic minorities.

Whether the decline of civility is real or not, there is certainly a notable, perhaps even general, perception that the decline is indeed real. What connects many of the various views on civility's decline is the commitment that civility matters, politically and democratically. Here, Mount's (1973, p. 31) eloquent depiction remains relevant:

> In the flourishing city, civility is part of the air we breathe. We no more trouble to analyse it than we take a chemical sample of the atmosphere when we lean out of the window on a summer morning. The mere presence of a debate on civility is therefore a sign that the city is in danger—or at least that people fear so.

We must be careful, though, not to misrepresent the *extent* of incivility in contemporary political discourse. Empirical data that unequivocally demonstrates that civility has declined is difficult to find, not least because the nature of political discourse has changed and proliferated in the digital, online age. In fact, while the development and widespread use of social media have been roundly identified by many as having played a crucial role in cultivating the "plight of civility", even here evidence is mixed. Analysing incivility in online political discussions in website and Facebook comments, Rowe (2015, p. 129) argues, for example, that "in line with previous research, the majority of comments in our sample were neither uncivil nor impolite". Of Rowe's analysis of 498 website comments, only 30 (6%) evidenced incivility, as did only 13 (2.7%) of Facebook comments. Earlier research by

---

[10] Calhoun (2000, p. 251), for example, starts her often cited article, *The Virtue of Civility* by asserting "the decline of civility". This assertion is also made by Edyvane (2017), who seems to equate the *concern* that civility has declined with evidence that civility has *actually* declined. See also Tanaseni (2019) and Jacobs (2019).

Papacharissi (2004) drew similar conclusions about the comparatively limited extent of incivility online compared with expressions of civility.[11]

My intention in this book is *not* to answer the question of whether civility is in decline directly or decisively, even if such a task was possible (which I am not convinced it is). Given that there has never been a "golden age" of civility, I think it is sufficient to say more simply that we could use some more civility in public life—irrespective of whether it is or is not in decline. The more pressing, and I would suggest interesting, concerns about civility are to say something substantive about (1) what civility consists of in modern western democracies, (2) why civility is necessary for a healthy, functioning and just democracy and (3) how greater levels of civility can be cultivated. That, at least, is the task for the remainder of this book.

Defining Civility

Following others,[12] I conceive there to be, broadly speaking, two forms of civility that are not unconnected, but between which it is both necessary and useful to distinguish—*everyday civility* and *political civility*. Everyday civility conforms to civility's more common usage, and refers more generally to politeness, manners and courteousness as people interact with others on a daily basis as they go about their lives. Examples of everyday civility are driven by social norms and customs. In the UK, for example, these might include greeting neighbours and passers-by, opening a door for others, giving up one's seat on public transport, giving way to other travellers on the roads, observing local norms and customs for activities such as eating, drinking and shopping, and various other fairly mundane but nevertheless important social niceties. Examples of everyday incivility, on the other hand, might include ignoring local norms and customs, road rage, listening to loud music on public transport, using profanities in public spaces, and so on.

Political civility concerns how citizens encounter each other and exchange ideas and interests in the public sphere. The use of the term "political" here is intentionally wide, and refers to the various activities engaged in by citizens in the public domain. The scope of political civility therefore includes the various social associations to which citizens belong and in which they engage. Political civility places

---

[11] Both Papacharissi and Rowe acknowledge that there is no commonly agreed measure of civility/incivility, with Rowe (2015, p. 128) acknowledging that such a measure "remains elusive". In his study, Rowe employed a detailed coding scheme developed by Papacharissi (see both for the scheme).

[12] This way of understanding of civility as involving a "formal component" and "morally substantive component" was common, for example, within the Scottish Enlightenment (Boyd 2013). In his often cited exposition of civility, Edward Shils (1997, p. 339) posited two related types of civility: "civility as good manners or courtesy" and "civility as the virtue of civil society". In his account of political civility as an illusionist ideal, Zurn (2013) distinguishes between personal civility and political civility, whereas Curzer (2012a) uses the terms polite and political civility. Laden (2019, p. 9) terms the two "civility as politeness" and "civility as responsiveness".

particular responsibilities on citizens that are not necessarily in play with everyday civility. As a simple example and as examined in more detail in the chapters which follow, political civility requires that we stay engaged with and are attentive to those whose views and actions we fundamentally disagree with. In Chap. 2, I outline in more detail precisely what being engaged and attentive requires of citizens, and when uncivil responses might be justified, but for now it suffices to suggest that such a commitment to remain engaged and attentive does not play an important role in everyday civility, where it is very easy to see that we can move away from and seek to severely restrict or remove altogether any contact with those we find impolite, rude and ill-mannered. This is not to suggest that everyday civility and political civility are unrelated. Everyday civility might be understood as something of a prerequisite for political civility. Fairly obviously, possessing good manners and being courteous do provide some basic underpinnings (or at least a starting point) for political civility.

Properly understood, political civility comprises two distinct and related components. First and foremost, political civility concerns how citizens *conduct*[13] themselves in their interactions with others: whether they enter dialogue with a commitment to open-mindedness, listening to others, seeking common ground and empathising with the views of others, for example. In western democracies, civil conduct acts as a political and social "lubricant" (Edyvane 2017, p. 348). Secondly, and as many writers on civility point out, conduct is not all that political civility requires of citizens. Political civility also involves particular bonds and relationships between citizens, supporting the potential for stability within democratic communities. In this second sense, political civility is both dependent on and in turns fosters mutual *fellow-feeling* and *well-wishing* between citizens. Conceiving political civility as concerned with both conduct and relationships with fellow citizens reminds us (1) that civil conduct occurs within given social contexts and (2) that how citizens conduct themselves is shaped by how they understand their relationships. As Boyd (2006, p. 865) argues, "a sense that we are all part of one moral collectivity or public can only exist when we are in the habit of treating one another in ways that observe the formal conditions of civility".[14] In addition, the existence and operation of civil conduct or mutual fellow-feeling cannot be taken for granted, but must be cultivated and nurtured. A core strand, then, of the account of political civility and its role within democratic education that I seek to offer in this book is that while political civility is the property of individuals in the sense that being civil is something that individuals do (or indeed do not do), civility only makes sense within a wider social context in which mutual well-being and fellow-feeling are valued, supported and encouraged.

---

[13] I am not claiming that the identification of these two components is original. Edyvane (2017), for example, focuses on civil conduct and civil attitude.

[14] As I touch upon at various points of this book, in contemporary, plural times the notion of a singular moral collectivity is not synonymous with the homogeneity of small-scales states. Moral collectivity in large heterogeneous democracies is suggestive of a more general form of social cooperation and, in actuality, takes differentiated forms across different contexts.

civil seems fairly obvious and uncontentious. In addition, and on a general level, tolerance furnishes civil conduct in the public domain with an awareness within citizens that they are able and free to make clear their own interests and convictions but accept that these interests and convictions can be openly and freely disputed by other citizens, so long as this occurs "in good faith" (Haldane 2019, p. 211). However, and more precisely, some further thinking is necessary to understand how tolerance and civility are connected. Given that both tolerance and civility are open to different conceptualisations, we must always ask what form of tolerance, and indeed what form of civility, we are speaking of.

The connection between civility and tolerance can be constituted in various ways. In his account of civility in the 1970s, Michael Walzer (1974, p. 601) presents tolerance as a "crucial form of civility", positioning tolerance as the more practical and possible way of living with diversity in large societies. Here, and contra to the reading of civility I offer in Chap. 3, Walzer contrasts tolerance with civic friendship in the following terms:

> We expect citizens to be tolerant of one another. This is probably as close as we can come to that "friendship" which Aristotle thought should characterize relations among members of the same political community. For friendship is only possible within a relatively small homogeneous city, but toleration reaches out infinitely.

In the next chapter, I say much more about both why I think civic friendship *is* possible in larger societies and how civic friendship relates to civility. For the present, the task at hand is to focus on tolerance and to argue that if civility does involve tolerance it requires both a particular, engaged form of tolerance and also extends beyond "being tolerant" on some simplistic or generalised account.[2]

An important theme within various philosophical, anthropological, sociological and theological accounts of civility is that civility requires *more* than a general sense of tolerance in which citizens with different standpoints co-exist within a given political community, but do so in a *disinterested* way. Disinterested in this sense means that while citizens are not incognisant of different interests and ways of living, they have no real engagement with or curiosity in those differences. The form of tolerance is, therefore, passive and generally speaking reflects a segregated way of living alongside but not *with* others. While disinterested, passive tolerance may well be important in certain situations (as discussed below), generally speaking, that kind of civility is one that fails to really grapple with the substance of politics—addressing and accommodating difference in democratic ways that resist factionalism and entrenched divisions—and that increasingly restricts contested and controversial viewpoints to the private realm.

This disinterested form of tolerance is lucidly captured by Elijah Anderson (2004, p. 15) in his account of life in a big urban city. Anderson describes public

---

[2] Deeper forms of tolerance, such as that offered by Scanlon (1996) or Samuel Scheffler (2010) are closer to the form of civility I am seeking to offer than other, more passive forms of toleration. For an extended discussion of these understandings of tolerance in relation to civility, see Edyvane (2017b).

Civility as a Civic Virtue

Throughout this book, in particular in Chaps. 2 and 3, I present civility as a civic virtue. Broadly conceived, civic virtues are worthwhile traits of character necessary for and expressed within social and political associations. As such, civic virtues are particular traits of character that enable citizens to participate well within their democratic community and which, in turn, enable communities to flourish. As with civic virtues more generally, being civil in the political sense involves thinking, feeling, deliberating and choosing the civil course of action in the particular situation in which one is involved. In this way, civility is context dependent, requiring that the individual agent first discerns the salient features of the situation, then contemplates these before arriving at and enacting an appropriate response. In addition, the option must always be open to perceive that civility is *not* the right course of action in the given situation. In later chapters, for example, I will suggest that there are limits to civility and that part of the wisdom required by the civil agent to discern when other, "uncivil" responses are necessary (in making this suggestion, certain conditions will be offered that might be used to judge when situations call for *justified incivility*).

The task of appraising the correct (civil) course of action in any given situation is not, of course, necessarily straightforward. Of help in this regard is Howard Curzer's (2012a) *Aristotelian Account of Civility,* considered in more detail in Chap. 2, in which he argues persuasively that civility operates as a means between two vices—incivility (the deficiency) and unfailing civility (the excess). According to Curzer (2012a, p. 84) "Civil people act and feel rightly when encountering people espousing differences". Note here that being civil requires right action and right feeling. While the right feelings associated with civility clearly include feeling appropriate levels of, for example, anger and frustration, in the sense that being overly angry may lead to uncivil responses and being insufficiently angry to unfailing civility, the connection between right action and right feeling serves further to remind us that civility is concerned with both the conduct of citizens and how citizens understand themselves as part of a wider, mutually regarding community. As I have mentioned above, and will examine in Chap. 3, while civility in modern, large democracies may often operate at a distance, civility cannot thrive if citizens view themselves as unattached and unconnected from their fellow citizens.

Before moving on, there are two final points of clarification that are important to make from the outset. First, in suggesting that civility, properly understood, is a vital civic virtue for contemporary democracies the claim I am making is not that civility can solve *all* of democracy's discontents. A healthy, functioning, just and inclusive democracy requires much more than civility alone can provide. My argument instead is that healthy, functioning, just and inclusive democracies require certain mechanisms that enable the mediation of different ideas and interests. These mechanisms are needed precisely to avoid factionalism and to furrow a path somewhere between perpetual conflict, forced homogeneity and the living of segregated lives. Civility is crucial for such a path. Without civility, democracy will be impoverished, if it is possible at all. Yet, and as I hope to attend to in the chapters that follow, there is a need to remain vigilant regarding how and when civility as a mechanism for mediating different ideas and interests is open to abuse to further subjugate and dominate groups already marginalised and disadvantaged. While civility alone cannot address major structural issues and inequalities—it is not a complete substitute for justice—when civility actually operates it may well help to support the cause of justice through enabling the interests of marginalised and disadvantaged groups to be publicised and heard.

Second, and as Cheshire Calhoun (2000) suggests, a prerequisite for any account of civility as an identifiably and meaningfully distinct virtue is to convince that civility is not reducible to other related concepts and virtues—such as tolerance, agreeableness and respect. Calhoun (2000, p. 259) frames the challenge particularly well, asserting that:

> Lists of political and polite civil behavior do not appear to depend on a prior understanding of civility as a distinct virtue. Instead, they appear to be entirely derived from a prior understanding of tolerance, considerateness, mutual respect, and a sense of justice. The question, "What should a civil person do?" appears to be interchangeable with the questions "How should mutually respectful citizens treat each other?" or "How should considerate social participants treat each other?" or "What does being tolerant of others' differences involve?"

Throughout this book, a number of terms clearly and closely associated with civility will be considered. It is my intention—or at least my hope—that when examining these related terms the precise relationship with civility held by each will be made clear and that, in so doing, the value of civility as a *distinct* virtue for public life will be elucidated. Part of my contention here, set out in detail in Chap. 3, is that civility is one of the core ways that citizens in contemporary western democracies enact and display civic friendship understood broadly as a sense of fellow-feeling and mutual well-wishing. In turn, when citizens understand themselves as friends in this civic sense, civility is further nourished. Of course, civility involves (in certain ways) being respectful, tolerant and agreeable with one's fellow citizens, but none of these terms alone fully depict what civility entails.

The Structure of this Book

Following this first, introductory chapter, the book is structured around three main chapters and a concluding chapter. Chapter 2 examines the first of the two components of civility identified above—civil conduct. In doing so, it focuses on the connections between civility and (1) tolerance and (2) deliberation. In addition, and drawing on Curzer's work on civility as an Aristotelian virtue, the analysis offered explores the boundaries of civility, including tentatively setting out some conditions for justified incivility (Curzer 2012b). Chapter 3 concentrates on the second of the two components of civility—civility and mutual fellow-feeling. Drawing links between civility and civic friendship, an argument is made that civility is both supported by, and in turn sustains, civic friendship. Attention is also paid to how the work and operation of formal and informal institutions and processes can serve to educate civility and, for that matter, incivility.

Chapter 4 offers some thoughts about how schools might cultivate civility as a key part of democratic education through educating pupils to situate civility, experience civility and enact civility. While I leave the explicit focus on schooling to this chapter, it is not the case that the analysis offered of civility in the preceding chapters stands in isolation from educational concerns. Given schools are a microcosm of society, many of the issues and concerns within wider societies mirror and impact upon what goes on in schools. The concluding chapter draws together the main themes and arguments of the book, before offering some thoughts about pressing research questions facing those interested cultivating civility in and through democratic education.

Through these chapters, I suggest that civility is a key way that citizens enact democracy based on mutual fellow-feeling and partnership. On this reading, civility in the public realm is not only about how citizens conduct themselves, but also about what citizens can reasonably expect of others within their political communities. An examination of civility necessarily engages us in some of the central questions of political life today, including how we recognise, build and sustain positive relationships which enable us to live alongside one another in diverse, heterogeneous communities? My suggestion in the remainder of this book is not that civility provides the only answer to such questions, but rather that it provides a crucial and compelling part of the answers.

References

American Psychological Association. (2018, October 5). *Panel discusses nation's decline in civil discourse.* Retrieved June 20, 2019, from https://www.apa.org/members/content/civil-discourse

Barrett, H. (1991). *Rhetoric and civility: Human development, narcissism, and the good audience.* Albany, NY: SUNY Press.

Bejan, T. M. (2017). *Mere civility: Disagreement and the limits of toleration.* Cambridge, MA: Harvard University Press.

Bloom, A. (1987). *The closing of the American mind.* New York: Simon & Schuster.

Boatright, R. G., Shaffer, T. J., Sobieraj, S., & Goldthwaite Young, D. (2019). *A crisis of civility? Political discourse and its discontents.* New York: Routledge.

Boyd, R. (2006). The value of civility. *Urban Studies, 43*(5/6), 863–878.

Boyd, R. (2013). Adam Smith on civility and civil society. In C. J. Berry, M. P. Paganell, & C. Smith (Eds.), *The Oxford handbook of Adam Smith.* Oxford: Oxford University Press.

British Broadcasting Corporation. (2019, February 2). *American civility: Year zero.* Archive on 4, First broadcast.

Calhoun, C. (2000). The virtue of civility. *Philosophy & Public Affairs, 29*(3), 251–275.

Carter, S. L. (1998). *Civility: Manners, morals and the etiquette of democracy.* New York: Basic Books.

Cohen, M. A. (2018). https://www.bostonglobe.com/opinion/2018/06/26/who-blame-for-american-civility-crisis/RQ4Pwip3kmUzuWeHRcNeIL/story.html

Curzer, H. J. (2012a). An Aristotelian account of civility. In D. S. Mower & W. L. Robison (Eds.), *Civility in politics and education.* New York: Routledge.

Curzer, H. J. (2012b). *Aristotle and the virtues*. Oxford, UK: Oxford University Press.

Edyvane, D. (2017). The passion for civility. *Political Studies Review, 15*(3), 344–354.

Fiala, A. (2013). The fragility of civility: Virtue, civil society, and tragic breakdowns of civility. *Dialogue and Universalism, 3*, 109–122.

Griffith, P., Norman, W., O'Sullivan, C., & Ali, R. (2011). *Charm offensive: Cultivating civility in 21st century Britain*. Retrieved February 19, 2019, from https://youngfoundation.org/wp-content/uploads/2012/10/Charm-Offensive-October-2011.pdf

Gümplová, P. (2016, March 10). The tragedy of Cologne and its aftermath – the depletion of civility. *Open Democracy*. Retrieved July 17, 2019, from https://www.opendemocracy.net/en/can-europe-make-it/tragedy-of-cologne-and-its-aftermath-depletion-of-civility/

Jacobs, J. (2019). Moral education, skills of civility, and virtue in the public sphere. In J. Arthur (Ed.), *Virtues in the public sphere: Citizenship, civic friendship and duty* (pp. 39–50). London: Routledge.

Jamieson, K. H., Volinsky, A., Weitz, I., & Kenski, K. (2015). The political uses and abuses of civility and incivility. In K. H. Jamieson & K. Kenski (Eds.), *The Oxford handbook of political communication*. Oxford, UK: Oxford University Press.

Kurti, P. (2018, July 5). Civility is on the decline and we all bear responsibility. *Australian Broadcasting Corporation*. Retrieved July 17, 2019, from https://www.abc.net.au/news/2018-07-05/sarah-hanson-young-david-leyonhjelm-civility-in-australia/9935110

Laden, A. S. (2019). Two concepts of civility. In R. G. Boatright, T. J. Shaffer, S. Sobieraj, & D. Goldthwaite Young (Eds.), *A crisis of civility? Political discourse and its discontents* (pp. 9–30). New York: Routledge.

Marquand, D. (2004). *Decline of the public: The hollowing out of citizenship*. Cambridge, MA: Polity Press.

Mount, F. (1973). The recovery of civility. *Encounter, XLI*, 31–43.

Nehring, H. (2011). 'Civility' in history: Some observations on the history of the concept. *European Review of History-Revue européenne d'histoire, 18*(3), 313–333.

Papacharissi, Z. (2004). Democracy online: Civility, politeness, and the democratic potential of online political discussion groups. *New Media & Society, 6*, 259–283.

Phillips, T., & Stuart, H. (2019). An age of incivility: Understanding the new politics. *Policy Exchange*. Retrieved July 17, 2019, from https://policyexchange.org.uk/wp-content/uploads/2018/11/An-Age-of-Incivility-Hannah-Stuart-and-Trevor-Phillips-Policy-Exchange-November-2018.pdf

Putnam, R. (2000). *Bowling alone: The collapse and revival of American community*. New York: Simon & Schuster.

Rowe, I. (2015). Civility 2.0: A comparative analysis of incivility in online political discussion. *Information, Communication & Society, 18*(2), 121–138.

Santana, A. D. (2014). Virtuous or vitriolic: The effect of anonymity in online newspaper reader comment boards. *Journalism Practice, 8*(1), 18–33.

Sennett, R. (2003). *The fall of public man*. London: Penguin.

Shils, E. (1997). *The virtue of civility: Selected essays on liberalisms, tradition and civil society*. Carmel, IN: Liberty Fund.

Tanaseni, A. (2019). Reducing arrogance in public debate. In J. Arthur (Ed.), *Virtues in the public sphere: Citizenship, civic friendship and duty* (pp. 28–38). London: Routledge.

Thomas, K. (2018). *In pursuit of civility: Manners and civilization in early modern England*. New Haven, CT: Yale University Press.

Walzer, M. (1974). Civility and civic virtue in contemporary America. *Social Research, 41*(4), 593–611.

Ward, I. (2017). Democratic civility and the dangers of niceness. *Political Theology, 18*(2), 115–136.

Zurn, C. F. (2013). Political civility: Another illusionistic ideal. *Public Affairs Quarterly, 27*(4), 341–368.

Chapter 2
Civil Conduct: Tolerance, Deliberation and the Possibility of "Justified Incivility"

Abstract This chapter focuses on the first component of political civility introduced in the previous chapter—civil conduct. Arguing for the importance of civil conduct and setting out of what civil conduct consists, the analysis involves a number of steps. The chapter begins with some preliminary remarks about civility and civic conduct. These remarks concentrate on clarifying the difference between manners as part of everyday civility and the sort of conduct required by political civility. The focus then moves more substantively to examine the relationships between, first, political civility and tolerance and, second, political civility and deliberation. It is argued that tolerance and political civility are connected, though distinct, concepts and that part of civil conduct involves discerning what form of tolerance is required by the given situation at hand. Connections are then drawn between political civility and deliberation, and here it is contended that civil deliberation must be cognisant of and seek to redress structural power inequalities if it is to be democratic, inclusive and just. The chapter also works to draw out some boundaries of political civility, and a tentative case is made for certain conditions under which incivility might be justified.

Keywords Civility · Civil conduct · Tolerance · Deliberation · Justified incivility

Introduction

In the introductory chapter, it was suggested that civility in its political sense comprises two interconnected components. The focus of this chapter is the first of these two components—civil conduct. In broad terms, civil conduct involves the manner in which citizens interact with other citizens in the public realm, but it runs much deeper than "manners". Civil conduct involves a set of capacities and dispositions that enable citizens to engage with each other, including being able to share one's

A. Peterson, *Civility and Democratic Education*, SpringerBriefs in Education, https://doi.org/10.1007/978-981-15-1014-4_2

13

own interests, to listen to the interests of others, to seek an appropriate accommodation of conflicting interests, to be open-minded, to eschew dogmatism and coercion and to enact an engaged form of tolerance.

The plan for the chapter, which consists of two main sections, is as follows. The first section begins with some preliminary remarks about civility and civic conduct. These remarks concentrate on clarifying the difference between manners as part of everyday civility and the sort of conduct required by political civility. The section moves more substantively to examine the relationships between, first, political civility and tolerance and, second, civility and deliberation. The second section aims to draw out some of the crucial boundaries of civility, including if and when it incivility might be justified. Drawing on Curzer's (2012) work on civility as a virtue, a case is made that under certain conditions—namely, where particular groups and their interests are systematically and structurally denied a place at the political table—incivility can be justified. In other words, justified incivility can act to make public deeply held outrage at persistent injustice.

A quick note before we proceed with this analysis. In this chapter and the remainder of the book, I use the terms "citizen" and "citizens" in a wide and general, rather than a formal legal, sense. Citizen/citizens refer to individuals and groups who inhabit a given political community, including elected officials, the general populace, and include those who, while not necessarily being afforded legal citizenship, nevertheless live in and participate within their communities. In this sense, being a citizen manifests itself in activities, actions and engagement within social and political associations, meaning both that people can hold multiple citizenships (determined, for example, by particular geographical and/or cultural influences) and can understand their citizenship/s as being fluid and contested.

Civility and Civil Conduct

My aim in this section is twofold. The first aim is to suggest that while manners as politeness are important for everyday civility, these are not all we have in mind when we are concerned with civil conduct, politically speaking. The second aim is to examine what is involved in civil conduct and to say something of the demands that such conduct places upon citizens. This latter aim is taken up through considering tolerance and deliberation in turn.

Let us start with the first of these two aims, and do so by considering what manners mean for everyday civility. Clearly, so far as everyday civility is concerned, manners are crucial. It would also be fair to say that what count as manners—what is deemed polite, what is deemed acceptable, etc.—is fashioned in and by specific contexts. In the context in which I write, the neighbour who says hello each morning might be viewed as civil, but this is not what civility means in a democracy nor what a democracy demands of those who are civil. If I am a civil neighbour, saying good morning, not playing music too loud or housing noisy pets, and keeping my garden clean and tidy are the most that can reasonably be *demanded* of me. Of course, being a "good" neighbour may involve more. Good neighbours might lend each other electrical items, keep parcels safe when the other is out, water plants when each other is away and so on. Moreover, and perhaps more importantly, they may engage in conversation, showing interest in each other's lives, families and so on. However, while these may represent what consists of being a "good" neighbour, it would be difficult to see how acting in the more limited way of being polite and courteous, though not being engaged in any deeper sense than this, could be considered bad or, indeed, uncivil.

While manners are shaped by particular social norms and customs—what might be polite in one context may be impolite in another—everyday civility certainly asks of us that we show some basic level of respect to others and that we show them common decency in and through our interactions. This is one of the central reasons why civility is relational—people showing respect and decency while receiving respect and decency from others. As Hume (1985, p. 89) once remarked, "in order to render conversation, and the intercourse of minds more easy and agreeable, good-manners have been invented". However, the potential murky relationship between manners and civility is not hard to see. That this is so can be illustrated with recourse again to Hume (1985, p. 87) and his contention that "[A]mong the arts of conversation, no one pleases more than mutual deference or civility, which leads us to resign our own inclinations to those of our companion, and to curb and conceal that presumption and arrogance, so natural to the human mind". The idea that civility involves curbing—and, perhaps worse, concealing—ourselves can be viewed in positive and negative lights. Viewed positively, civility involves a humility and an absence of dogmatism when advancing our interests and viewpoints and an attentiveness which allows us to not only hear the interests of others, but to also work consciously in an effort to make others comfortable in sharing their interests with us. Viewed negatively, civility requires a superficial form of manners through which we hide and mask our true commitments. Also, and as Kristjánsson (2006, p. 33) forcefully contends:

> The very words "manners" and "etiquette" typically conjure up an air of sanctimoniousness, bigotry, hideboundedness, and more generally, of morally irrelevant rules that have congealed into banal formalities.

In a useful distinction, Ward (2017, p. 119; emphasis in original) distinguishes between the "*virtue* of civility and its *semblance*" of niceness, and suggests that we must accept that outward expressions of civility are open to manipulation and pretence (an issue to which I return at various points in this book). Simply put, we must be aware that acting civilly may be nothing more than a veneer, and that someone's speaking politely and conforming to social norms may be a façade; that is, a means to some other end. In general terms, and without much further elaboration and qualification, manners are neither particularly political nor indeed moral. As Comte-Sponville (2001) reminds us, the problem when manners do not run deep is not that the manners are absent but that the manners might be deliberately employed to mask vice/s. A key concern with viewing civility as synonymous with manners and in largely behavioural terms, then, is that such a conception presents a "thin and watery virtue—all surface presentation and no content" (Kelly 2018, p. 199). The sort of political engagement and interaction likely to result will be narrow and shallow, or will lead to "a discourse that is so polite and restrained that it is barely human" (Papacharissi 2004, p. 266).

These concerns noted, there does seem to be some truth in the suggestion that manners and political civility may in some way be connected. Certainly, it would be difficult to see how a person with political civility would not be attentive in some important ways to the manners required and expected in a particular context. Further, and as perhaps most famously contended by Erasmus in *De Civilitate*[1], manners can be a sign and outward expression of inner virtues. However, a notion of political civility that rests on forms of conduct that could be viewed as sterile or sanctimonious or routine or banal and so on would be fatally insecure and unsubstantial. To be meaningful, political civility must place more rigorous demands on the conduct of citizens than manners alone. But what are these demands?

Unlike the civil neighbour, where the demands of everyday civility are comparatively light, civil conduct requires a deeper form of engagement with others, including with others whom hold different perspectives and interests. These different perspectives and interests may, of course, be in conflict. It is at least in part for this reason that civility in its political sense has been connected to a number of related, and not dissimilar, terms—most notably tolerance, but also other terms such as respect, open-mindedness and humility. Obtaining clarity about the relationship between civility (from now on I return in this chapter to using civility as shorthand for political civility) and related notions such as respect and tolerance is not helped by the fact that some analyses conflate the concepts, adopting the view that civility really just amounts to "a cluster of other more basic attitudes such as 'tolerance', 'considerateness' or 'respect'" (Edyvane 2017a, p. 348; see also Boyd 2006; Edyvane 2017b; for an insightful discussion of tolerance as a way of responding to discord in public debate, see Haldane 2019).

If we focus in particular on tolerance, which is my intention here, any worthwhile account of civility needs to be clear and precise as to how civility connects with and extends beyond tolerance as it is through understanding these connections and extensions that the demands civility places on citizens can be clarified, thereby helping to flesh out an appropriate form of civility for contemporary democratic life. My argument in the paragraphs that follow will be that while tolerance is a core element of civility, it is not a direct synonym. Part of the reason why civility extends beyond tolerance is attended to in the next chapter. Here, I wish to consider how and why tolerance, of a particular kind, is indeed part of civil conduct.

Civility and Tolerance

Civility clearly does relate in important ways to tolerance, and it seems reasonable to suggest that tolerance of some form is inherent in what we understand civility to be in practical terms. The statement that a citizen who is intolerant is unlikely to be

---

[1] Nehring (2011).

spaces as locations in which "pedestrians move about guardedly, dealing with strangers by employing elaborate facial and eye work, replete with smiles, nods, and gestures geared to carve out an impersonal but private zone for themselves" (ibid.). Anderson continues, "in navigating such spaces, people often divert their gazes, looking up, looking down, or looking away, and feign ignorance of the diverse mix of strangers they encounter" (ibid.). Anderson (2004, p. 15; emphasis in original) compares this way of living with difference with contrasting spaces in which citizens engage "under a virtual *cosmopolitan canopy*" where people "treat others with a certain level of civility" and "where instantaneous communities of diverse strangers emerge and materialize". Recounting vignettes of engagements with difference afforded by the cosmopolitan canopy, Anderson (2004, p. 25) sums up their value:

> Essentially, cosmopolitan canopies allow people of different backgrounds the chance to slow down and indulge themselves, observing, pondering, and in effect, doing their own folk ethnography… An accretion of such shared observations made under the cosmopolitan canopies of the city becomes part of what people "know" about each other, a way they "make sense" of the more public world.

As Walzer (1974, p. 602) notes, a core issue for liberal forms of tolerance is the extent to which the passive accommodation of difference is "antithetical to political activism" precisely because it promotes "among citizens a general indifference toward the opinions of their fellows". In contrast, the form of tolerance that civility—at least the account of civility I am offering—requires is an *interested* form of tolerance characterised by various degrees of active and critical engagement with the ideas, beliefs and interests of one's fellow citizens. One way of understanding this form of tolerance and how it connects to civility is to contrast it with the helpful account of tolerance and civility offered by Derek Edyvane (2017b). Edyvane's aim is to distinguish certain versions of tolerance from civility. He contends that:

> While negative toleration is the name we typically give to accommodation *in spite* of differences of values, identities and customs, and toleration as recognition is the name we give to accommodation *because* of such differences (or at least in recognition of them), I suggest that we think of civility as accommodation *irrespective* of difference. That is to say, we can think of civility as a mode of accommodation in which parties to the practice simply set aside their differences, instead of negatively supressing or positively affirming them (2017b, p. 466; emphasis in original).

Conscious of the fact that some critics of tolerance are concerned that citizens might be expected to suppress their differences with others (endangering their own sense of worth and values), Edyvane (2017b) clarifies what it means to "set aside our differences". When differences are set aside "we come to regard them or decide to treat them as not being pertinent to the matter at hand. We may still think of them as being important; we simply cease to see them as bearing fundamentally on the context in question". What Edyvane seems to have in mind is a form of civility in which differences between individuals, groups and factions are put to one side in pursuit of the common, collective interest; that is, in which differences are understood as important, but are just not viewed as being particularly relevant.

While I find Edyvane's position insightful and instructive for the extent to which it critiques negative tolerance and questions limited forms of recognising difference,

I think it underplays three core considerations. The first of these considerations is that the choice *not* to set aside differences of values, identities and customs is not always and necessarily a feature of *in*civility. As Zurn (2013, p. 349) argues, "civility is perfectly consistent with 'taking a principled stand', being unwilling to compromise or agree with opponents, ideological rigidity, supporting one's own political 'team', and maintaining party discipline". Put simply, my concern with setting aside important differences, even if this were psychologically possible, is that it seems to require that citizens divest themselves of much of what makes them human and gives shape and meaning to their viewpoints and actions in the public sphere.

The second consideration, and as I have alluded to above, is that the setting aside of differences seems to be based on a particular understanding of liberal democratic life in which the scope of both participation and the political community is reasonably limited and in which the distinction between private and public realms is sharp. This understanding focuses too narrowly, and diminishes the varied and wide nature of political communities and the real substance of democratic politics. As Michael Sandel (1996) reminds us, "democratic politics, properly conducted, is filled with controversy". Conflict is crucial to what makes democracies necessary and functional. As a default mechanism, civility must facilitate the conditions under which difference can be engaged with and just accommodation of different interests sought, while maintaining social cooperation. In addition, the scope of political civility must be wide, and take in the variety of interactions and associations that comprise political and civil society. Dealing with difference and conflicting interests and values is necessary for the stability of democratic projects, requiring "citizens who are skilled in the arts of self-government—deliberation, compromise, consensus-building, civility, reason-giving" (Glendon 1995, p. 4). This point seems to be particularly important for modern, plural democracies in which different conceptions of precisely what is in the collective interest are evident.

The third consideration is that prioritising the setting aside of differences appears to overlook the fact that the form of tolerance required for civility has to be informed and guided by the particularities of the given context and situation. It is only when we have engaged with others (historically and/or recently) and felt the effects of such engagement that we are in a position to ascertain that a more productive outcome would simply be to set aside our differences. In other words, when civility is understood as an intermediate mean between an excess and a deficiency this entails that a range of options are available to citizens when they engage with diverse interests. To be civil, therefore, requires appraising, discerning and judging when and why setting differences aside may be possible and fruitful and, indeed, when and why a more passive form of tolerance can provide a more pragmatic response than engagement with differences (the educational relevance of this point is examined in Chap. 4).

I think this latter point that any setting aside of differences can only really be meaningfully enacted following a fuller engagement *with* these differences is worthy of more examination. To be clear, my contention is that when an individual citizen or group of citizens choose a particular form of tolerance in order to be civil, what makes the choice civil or not is not solely down to the conceptualisation of tolerance (i.e. tends towards passivity or tends towards engagement) and approach to difference (i.e. suppression, recognition or setting aside) invoked. In addition to these, the appropriate form of tolerance must correspond to the salient features of the situation at hand. Just as Zurn (2013, p. 348) contends that "civility is itself democratically reflexive: a society's current, conventional standards of civil discourse are themselves open to democratic debate, discussion and change", so too civility requires the citizen to be individually reflexive, opening their minds to ways of being tolerant that are responsive to historical, cultural and political factors at play.

To understand civility in this way includes an appreciation that an interested and engaged form of tolerance is of a more demanding and risky kind than then more passive forms, and, crucially, that in certain situations a more passive form of tolerance is precisely what civility requires. The sorts of situations I have in mind are those in which relationships between groups and individuals are sensitive or fraught and in which any deeper form of engagement with difference is likely to lead to inflamed conflict, thereby destabilising the political community. In her anthropological study conducted in post-war Jaffna, Sri Lanka, Thiranagama depicts the fragility in which civility and tolerance exists. Thiranagama (2018, p. 358) presents a vivid description of her encounter with an older woman selling peanuts to support herself outside a church in Jaffna. The woman's son had been killed by the Sri Lankan army during the civil war, and her husband had subsequently killed himself. Describing interactions with her Muslim neighbours, the women explained that now "'there was no problem with Muslims'... 'You see,' she said 'a lot of contact/familiarity (*sontam*) brings lots of problems, little familiarity brings no problems... otherwise little fights will become big fights'". In other words, passivity and refraining from closer engagement were judged to be the appropriately civil response in that particular situation, and that particular time.

Not dissimilar findings are reported from other conflict/post-conflict contexts. In their study of young mothers in post-peace agreement Belfast, Smyth and McKnight (2013) draw on Goffman's notion of "civil inattention" to examine the lived experiences and choices of the mothers in the daily lives. They found that "participants in deeply divided societies respond to anxieties about potential conflict in everyday life through strategies which are aimed at blending in with their surrounding contexts, and thereby avoiding drawing attention to themselves" (2013, p. 316). Through enacting civil inattention, the participants were able to go about their lives. Also writing about post-peace agreement Belfast, Lepp (2018) speaks of the importance of shared spaces (his study examines the example of the SSE Arena, the home of the Belfast Giants Ice Hockey team) within which differences remain obscured, but within which commonalities can gently be formed. Such social spaces may well turn out to be a stepping stone on the journey towards greater interaction, as according to Lepp (2018, p. 42) "the hockey arena has normalised this secure place to stand, manufacturing a sense of acceptance in being side by side that has yet to emerge as normal in wider Belfast". In this way, forms of civility sensitive to and shaped by historical context are helping to "articula[te] new relationships of citizenship" (Jeffrey and Staeheli 2015, p. 2). What seems to be notable in each of these examples is that the people living in these contexts are making considered and reflexive judgements about what civility requires that are sensitive to recent and historical tensions, discerning what an intermediate course between incivility and unfailing civility might be. In other words, civil inattention seems to work when it is logically informed by the given cultural and political contexts.

The purpose of this section so far has been to begin the task of arguing and demonstrating why civil conduct involves but extends beyond manners and politeness. The argument made has been twofold: First, that while manners are necessary for political civility, they are not sufficient because equating political civility with manners runs the risk of civil conduct being superficial, fleeting and insincere and thus masking political vices. Second, that part of the reason political civility extends beyond manners is that politically civil conduct involves an approach to tolerance that consists of an engagement *with* difference but which is also sensitive to salient features of a situation that inform when a more restricted form of tolerance would comprise the right course of action commensurate with an intermediate course of civility.

Civility and Deliberation

Further help in delineating the form of conduct political civility requires of citizens can be gained by examining the main tenets of deliberative forms of political discourse. Though not a homogenous field, certain features of deliberative democratic theory (and indeed practices) have close synergies with political civility, and as Calhoun (2000, p. 260) remarks, "civility is an essentially *communicative* form of moral conduct". This said, my focus on deliberative political encounters between citizens as a *primary* expression of civility should not be read as its only scope. Civility in contemporary democracies runs wider than political and social talk, and includes a more general conduct on the part of citizens to relate to each other and political institutions in mutually beneficial ways—including, as I have argued above, making the conscious choice to be inattentive in civic encounters. As Young (2000, p. 12) reminds supporters of deliberative democracy, "inclusion specifically requires openness to a plurality of modes of communication", a fact Smyth and McKnight (2013) highlight in their study of sectarianism and civility in Belfast. Nevertheless, it is *largely* through dialogic encounters that civility is enacted and experienced. Indeed, civility can be understood as a core prerequisite for deliberative democracy, central to its very meaning.[3] It is therefore beholden on any account of civility to be clear as to what civil deliberation involves. This, at least, will be my focus in the rest of this section.

---

[3] For example, Fishkin and Luskin (2005), Farrelly (2007) and Cohen (2012). See Mitchell (2018) for a brief overview.

Let us start with some general pronouncements about deliberative engagement, before becoming more specific. The following commitments, each grounded in recognising the active participation of citizens in deliberative processes, are central to deliberative democracy and democratic legitimacy. First, that such participation should extend beyond the regular, periodic election of representatives to positions of political power and authority. Second, that political participation should be largely enacted through discursive and dialogic processes that enable citizens to make their own interests (ideas, thoughts, beliefs, positions, etc.) known and through which they come to know and understand the interests of others (it is partly for this reason that deliberative democracy is based on reciprocity and mutual recognition). Third, that discursive and dialogic processes recognise mutual associations and should therefore facilitate deliberation between citizens (in both an individual and group sense) as well as between citizens and governments (whether local, regional or national). Fourth, that deliberative politics requires citizens to possess particular capacities—including civility—and these capacities must be cultivated through deliberative institutions and processes. And, fifth, that deliberative processes recognise and account for the inclusion of plural interests, including those of marginalised and disadvantaged groups (see, for example, Cohen 1997; Gutmann and Thompson 2004; Dryzek 2010). A critical feature of this latter commitment is, as Pettit (1997, p. 184) argues, that deliberative processes "track[s] the interests and the ideas" of citizens affected by decisions and policies.

Deliberative democracy places citizens as active agents in receiving and sharing interests with others—including, where appropriate, those with whom they fundamentally disagree. Indeed, and as I have suggested above, meaningful engagement with difference represents a core feature of contemporary democratic life that brings the need for civility to the fore. Civil deliberation does not mean, however, that disagreement and conflict will end; far from it. Speaking in late 2008 as President Elect about his decision to invite evangelical Pastor Rick Warren, Barack Obama[4] argued the following:

> It is no secret that I am a fierce advocate for equality for gay and lesbian Americans. It is something that I have been consistent on, and something that I intend to continue to be consistent on during my presidency. What I have also said is that it is important for America to come together, even though we may have disagreements on certain social issues… We are not going to agree on every single issue but what we have to do is be able to create an atmosphere where we can *disagree without being disagreeable* and then focus on those things we hold in common as Americans.

In this passage, Obama invokes the spirit of deliberative democracy through which community is nourished and sustained by citizens recognising their differences while coming "to appreciate and act upon the interests and values they share with their neighbors" (Jacobs et al. 2009, p. 12).

The existence of plural interests is a defining feature of modern western democracies. Recalling her father's views on the difference between a dictatorship and

---

[4] https://www.youtube.com/watch?v=syIEoSIJHis

democracy shaped by his experiences as a child during the Spanish civil war, Delgado (2018, p. 328) offers the following evocative and perceptive insight: "He had witnessed what a dictatorship does to human rights: families separated, dissidents tortured, individuals imprisoned without proper trials or appropriate legal representation. Democracies he believed were places where you could hold an alternative opinion and not risk public humiliation, imprisonment, torture or death for doing so". The existence of disagreement is a precondition of deliberative democracy so far as, firstly, that disagreement necessitates deliberation, secondly, that deliberation seeks to accommodate difference, and, thirdly, that deliberation seeks to reconcile difference. Yet, much ink has been spilled about the extent to which deliberation can genuinely, whether in intention or otherwise, offer hope of consensus and agreement (Gutmann and Thompson 2002; List 2017; Eriksen 2018). Indeed, according to some critics of deliberative democracy, the engagement with difference it requires will actually serve to heighten, rather than reduce, disagreement.[5] The premise of such criticisms is that by bringing plural interests into open discussion, many of which will be deeply held and/or sensitive, deliberative forums just serve to bring out deeper divisions. Even if it is the case that sharing our interests through deliberative means *can* lead to further disagreement and conflict (for example, in post-conflict contexts as suggested above) it is far from clear that it *always* does. For example, in their study of public deliberation in America, Jacobs et al. (2009, p. 76) found a correlation between the tendency of those facilitating discussions to "help the group to come to an agreement" and the commitment from discussants to "airing differences":

> We found no consistent and strong evidence that deliberation intensifies disagreement, as deliberation critics fear. In addition, the fear that deliberation suppresses disagreement is also not directly evident…Our findings suggest that disagreements have been aired even as face-to-face forums move toward finding areas of shared interests and concerns.

Similarly, the use of a citizens' assembly in Ireland in 2018 has been credited with arriving at a consensus over abortion laws. *The Guardian* (2018) reported the success of the assembly in the following way:

> Ninety-nine random strangers, a North Dublin hotel and a lot of cups of tea and coffee—not exactly the stuff of political revolution. Yet little more than a year later, it appears that an unlikely assemblage of housewives, students, ex-teachers, truck drivers and others has brought Ireland to the brink of radical change to its abortion laws. They met as a Citizens' Assembly at the end of 2016, a mix of pro-lifers, pro-choicers and undecideds whose views broadly reflected opinions in the wider Irish population. In all, it took five weekends. But at the end of it, they voted for change. In doing so, they did not just pave the way for an abortion referendum in May… They showed the world what democrats can do with a little imagination.

Faced with seemingly intractable and entrenched disagreement, the citizens' assembly was credited with breaking the deadlock and paving the way for a referendum. Broadcast on the internet, the meetings witnessed open and impassioned

---

[5] See, for example, Mansbridge (1983), Sulkin and Simon (2001).

discussion for and against changing (liberalising) Ireland's laws on abortion. According to the then deputy of Ireland's governing Fine Gael party, Kate O'Connell, "I think this issue, in Ireland, could never have gotten to the point we're at today, were it not for the citizens' assembly. I think we would have been years getting there, if we ever got there".

The example of the citizens' assembly in Ireland provides an illustration of how deliberation, conducted in civil ways, can enable not just an engagement with difference, but an engagement characterised by the willingness to co-operate, to be open-minded, to listen, to make clear passionate positions held, to engage with evidence and expertise, and to seek some form of agreement. In this particular case, it was this commitment and enactment of civil conduct that provided the oil needed to grease the deliberative interactions, reducing the chance that the gears would become fractious or become locked altogether. As Kingwell (1994, p. 211) suggests, civil exchanges involve "coaxing out the interests of others through sensitivity and tact". Returning to the findings reported by Jacobs et al. (2009, p. 82):

> Deliberators consistently reported that face-to-face forums were genuinely public spaces where a wide spectrum of the community could gather to talk about their shared interests and pursue broad areas of agreement. Deliberators did not report the kind of fixation with winning or losing an advantage that is sometimes attributed to American public life.

As I hope to have made clear by now, deliberative discourse depends on civil conduct characterised by opened-mindedness, passionate commitment free from dogmatism, giving and receiving a fair hearing, being clear on the complexities involved, and so on. In other words, and crucially, civil conduct requires that citizens are present with and are attentive to others, listening to their ideas and stories and seeking to empathise with them. Part of the problem when public discourse fails or becomes overly fractious is precisely because some or other citizen or group involved removes themselves from the discussion (physically or otherwise) and fails to be attentive to the interests of others. When conduct takes this form, particular citizens or groups—often, though not always those with less power—are denied their voice and their interests fail to be recognised. For this reason, showing a willingness to engage, listen and respond is crucial. Speaking in 2019 shortly after announcing his intention to stand for the leadership of the Conservative Party in the UK and in the context of deep divisions regarding the UK's withdrawal from the European Union, MP Rory Stewart explained that:

> I think that this is a very very courteous country, so a lot of the people I talk to will disagree with me very very strongly about Brexit. They will never want to vote for me, but people are very happy to have a rant at you and then shake hands and be very warm when you move on. I think basically people appreciate you being out there... the main thing people say is "thank god you're here, what bothers me is that you are here, that I can see you". So, listening, listening and acting.

My use of Stewart's reflections here should not be read as suggesting that *all* civic encounters are like this; there are countless, regular examples in which discussions between citizens and politicians are far from civil. Rather, it is to argue that civil conduct is hard work and can be demanding on citizens. Waldron (2013, p. 13) cites a perceptive statement from *The Institute for Civility in Government* that states "civility is the hard work of staying present even with those with whom we have deep-rooted and fierce disagreements", arguing further that "fierce political antagonism need not precipitate exit from the political process". As Nelson Mandela famously said, "if you want to make peace with your enemy, you have to work with your enemy. Then he becomes your partner".[6]

An example which occurred at the time of writing this book further illustrates the tensions and challenges involved in deciding when to "stay present" and attentive, and when to choose an alternative course. Democratic presidential candidate, and former Vice President, Joe Biden, provoked controversy when he would not apologise for working in the past with senators whom held and expressed racist views. Although Biden (BBC 2019) made clear that he "detested" the senators' views, he suggested that "At least there was some civility. We got things done. We didn't agree on much of anything. We got things done. We got it finished. But today, you look at the other side and you're the enemy. Not the opposition, the enemy. We don't talk to each other anymore" (Washington Examiner 2019). For some, including others running for the Democrat nomination, Biden's "civility" had led him to work with others with detestable views, or what fellow candidate Kamala Harris termed "praising" and "coddling" segregationists (BBC 2019). This brief, yet significant, vignette raises two significant questions. The first is when the dispositions to be attentive and present shift from being positive and worthwhile to being negative and weak; that is they become akin to unfailing civility. The second question is what other responses are appropriate when citizens are faced with situations in which remaining present and attentive are no longer a viable, virtuous option. In the next section, I seek to provide some responses to both of these questions.

The Limits of Civility: Or When Is It Justified to Be Uncivil?

Any theoretically robust and practically useful account of civility must attend to the vexed problem of when, if ever, it is morally justified to be uncivil. Various candidates exist for demarcating the boundaries of civil and uncivil action. Calhoun (2000), for example, identifies Gutmann and Thompson's (1990) principle of genuine moral positions as one potential candidate, offering as it does a critical normative account of the boundaries for political dialogue. According to Gutmann and Thompson, views which discriminate, such as defending racism, are not genuine moral positions and, therefore, do not require a civil response. Calhoun challenges such critical normative positions on the basis that they may serve to undermine a fundamental role played by civility in contemporary, heterogeneous political communities; namely, that civility helps citizens to engage with difference and controversial viewpoints, serving to moderate discussion in order that

---

[6] https://www.sanews.gov.za/south-africa/nelson-mandela-famous-quotes

these viewpoints may be expressed, engaged with and challenged. For Calhoun (2000, p. 269):

> Civility norms regulate discussion by requiring all parties equally to respond with respect toward the *same* set of positions that are on the table for discussion regardless of what they may privately think about those positions. In other words, civility norms bar dialogue participants from exercising their own individual judgement about what views are utterly contemptible, intolerable, and not worth a respectful hearing.

Calhoun has in mind two worries about the impact of resting the boundaries of civility on a given moral framework. If multiple moral frameworks are invoked (particularly at the level of individuals), the result will be "civility anarchy", with each individual or group of citizens deciding "for themselves where the bounds of civility are set" (Calhoun 2000, p. 270). Alternatively, if one single moral framework is at play, it is imposed as "the supreme legislator of what counts as legitimate critical morality" (p. 271). In either case, the role of civility in regulating political dialogue is, for Calhoun, undermined.

Rather than adopting some form of normative moral framework, Calhoun appeals instead to social consensus as a basis for delimiting civility and incivility. Referencing sexual harassment and racial discrimination as two areas commonly cited as not being owed a civil response, Calhoun (2000, p. 271) contends that "these are moral matters on which there is presently extensive social consensus (which is not to say unanimity)… We need not respond civilly to a view or behaviour once there is social closure on its intolerability. At that point, civility would not further the work of enabling the nonlike-minded to continue political dialogue or social interaction". Detailing the difference between her view and the appeal to normative moral frameworks, Calhoun (2000, p. 271) contends that "they assume that civility is a virtue we are required to exercise toward others only if those others pursue genuinely morally acceptable views and behavior", and offers the alternative "civility is a virtue that we are required to exercise toward others only if they pursue *socially* acceptable views and behaviour".

Although not wishing to rule out the importance of the sort of social consensus Calhoun favours (clearly, the degree of social consensus present on the topic at hand is one important consideration in whether views expressed deserve a civil response), I think we need to be careful about resting the boundaries of what views and positions are deserving of a civil response *solely* on social consensus. The two main reasons I have in mind may not necessarily be fatal to the sort position offered by Calhoun, but they are interesting to consider and are relevant to the focus of the remainder of this chapter.

The first concern is the tension that translating the idea of social consensus on the wrongness of, for example, racism into practice is unlikely to be straightforward in certain cases. Where racism is *obvious* and *blatant*, then clearly such views should not be responded to with civility. It is not altogether clear, however, that the boundaries of racist positions can be drawn so clearly in all cases. To draw on an illustrative case, views on immigration and particular migrants expressed by Nigel Farage during the lead-up to the UK's referendum on membership of the European Union have been described as racist by vocal opponents.[7] Writing in The Times, former chairman of the UK's Equalities and Human Rights Commission, Trevor Phillips contested such a reading of Farage's views, arguing that:

> In Farage's case, no one has yet found anything he said to warrant the oft-hurled label "racist". I don't think that Farage is personally hostile to people of colour. In my encounters with him I have found him to be more respectful and at ease with me than many of the left-wing intelligentsia who abhor him. One glance at the ethnic diversity of the Brexit Party's MEP candidates would put any Oxbridge senior common room to shame. And the more the allegation is made against him, the more it seems the real target of Remainer criticism isn't Farage but the ordinary voters who made the "wrong" choice in the referendum.

There seem to be two related concerns in Phillips' words. The first is that by focusing on the "character" of the individual, the difficulties with the precise nature and implications of their views and desired policies become obfuscated. The second is that labelling an interlocutor and their views as racist means that these views do not need to be engaged with any further, closing down rather than opening up discourse and deliberation. Unless there is clear and compelling evidence that a fellow citizen is prejudice or is expressing prejudice views, part of the price citizens have to pay might well be to hear and engage with views they do not find acceptable, seeking to clarify and challenge these, subject of course to laws and social norms around free speech and hate speech. To be clear given that this is such a critical point, this is not to suggest that any form of prejudice and discrimination *must* be tolerated and engaged with—a point I return to later in this section. As a range of historical and contemporary examples attest, persistent tensions exist between achieving an appropriate balance between free speech and protection from prejudice and hate, a process which involves a continual traversing of various concerns.[8] It is to suggest, however, that things are not always clear cut and we need some way of getting to grips with the nuances and complexities of views different to our own before we dismiss them outright. There has to be some room for citizens to use their own judgement, informed of course but not entirely guided by social consensus, about when civility is an appropriate and morally justifiable stance. As I return to in Chap. 4, this point seems particularly relevant for educating civility in schools. At a time when children are exploring their own views, clarifying these against other views, traversing the views of their parents, peers and teachers, making

---

[7] https://www.theneweuropean.co.uk/top-stories/femi-oluwole-debates-brexit-party-activist-1-6015344

[8] For example, in 2014, George Brandis, then Attorney-General of Australia argued in favour of the government's plan to amend the Australia's racial discrimination laws to repeal a section stating that it is unlawful to publicly "offend, insult, humiliate or intimidate" persons or groups. Brandis claimed that "people do have a right to be bigots. In a free country people do have rights to say things that other people find offensive or insulting or bigoted" (https://www.abc.net.au/news/2014-03-24/brandis-defends-right-to-be-a-bigot/5341552). Brandis' stance has been connected to the Federal Court decision in 2011 which ruled that journalist Andrew Bolt breached the Act in two articles that "implied that light-skinned people who identified as Aboriginal did so for personal gain" (https://www.abc.net.au/news/2011-09-28/bolt-found-guilty-of-breaching-discrimination-act/3025918)

mistakes and developing their vocabulary, judging whether their views are or are not racist or do or do not approximate to racism remains a highly complex and nuanced task.

The second concern is that social consensus seems a rather fluid and not wholly reliable measure of what counts as an acceptable view or otherwise. Plenty of instances can be identified in which social consensus has landed on the side of prejudice and discrimination, and continues to do so today. Social consensus just seems too insecure a foundation to alone provide the anchoring necessary for drawing the boundaries of civility. So too, we must be mindful that social consensus does not become shorthand for what the founder and director of the Academy of Ideas, Claire Fox (2018) has called the rise of "illiberal liberalism" through which some liberals repress viewpoints and debate through intolerance to alternatives. There is not scope in this book to enter into the extensive literature and practical examples of tensions about free speech and no-platforming on University-campuses (see, Mower and Robison's (2012) edited collection for some insightful analyses), but the very real hostilities involved give some cause for concern that appeals to social consensus are being used to shut down debates and silence ideas contra the liberalism of Rousseau, Locke and Mill. As Delgado (2018, p. 328) writes in her analysis of civility, empathy, democracy and memory, "dictatorships coerce; democracies converse"

Rather than social consensus per se, I would like to argue, following and building on Curzer's (2012) framing, that understanding civility as an intermediate mean between two extremes—the deficiency and the excess—is more helpful in drawing its limits and boundaries. Such a mean is clearly informed by central social considerations, including social norms, social contexts and degrees of social consensus, but goes beyond this in certain ways. With this in mind, the purpose of the remainder of this section is to respond to the two questions raised at the end of the previous section in order to understand, (1) what unfailing civility is and why it is problematic for public discourse and (2) what incivility is and to examine when being uncivil *can* be an appropriate and justified response, politically speaking.

The Excess and the Deficiency

Let us remind ourselves of what constitutes the excess and deficiency of civility. As suggested in the introduction to this book, in his *Aristotelian Account of Civility* Howard Curzer (2012, p. 84) defines civility as when people "act and feel rightly when encountering people espousing differences" and suggests that civility operates as a means between two vices—incivility (the deficiency) and unfailing civility (the excess). If we turn first to the excess, defining unfailing civility seems a fairly straightforward task. To be unfailingly civil is to conduct one's self with manners, to remain present, to listen and to be attentive without resorting to anger, insults or departing altogether *no matter what the provocation*. While some might view this as a sign of strength in the sense that the citizen with unfailing civility is durable, perseveres and keeps coming back for more, unfailing civility is more likely to be equated with someone weak of will, who is able to be pushed around by others, who is ingratiating, and is unable to stand-up to intolerable views or challenge injustices.

Turning to the deficiency, in its everyday sense incivility can be defined as rude, vulgar or unsociable speech and actions. In its political sense, incivility is more expansive and includes making personal slights and attacks, failing to treat others with dignity, boorish behaviour, telling deliberate falsehoods, and forms of prejudice and discrimination (racism, sexism, homophobia, Islamophobia and so on). In Chap. 4, I draw on a list of 12 manifestations of incivility identified by Phillips and Stuart (2018), which includes dehumanisation, misogyny and homophobia, racism and anti-Muslim prejudice, anti-Semitism and intimations and/or threats of violence. Useful definitions of incivility can also be found in recent literature on online political discussions, which typically understand incivility as referring to "features of discussion that convey an unnecessarily disrespectful tone toward the discussion forum, its participants, or its topics" (Coe et al. 2014, p. 660; see also, Galarza Molina and Jennings 2018). In her work on online political discussions, Papacharissi (2004) distinguishes between civility, incivility and impoliteness. Uncivil comments were those using threats or invoked negative stereotypes. By contrast, impolite comments were those which exhibited rudeness, name-calling and the like.

Of course, incivility can take destructive forms, including the use of physical violence. As Zurn (2013, p. 348, 349) contends, "civility is fundamentally opposed to the use of physical violence", but "does *not* exclude civil disobedience". As intimated earlier, we must also be mindful, too, that determinations of what counts as civil and uncivil can be politically motivated, with civility sometimes used as a tool for the powerful to constrain the actions and behaviour of those they oppress and marginalise (see, for example, Elias 2000). Richard Boyd (2006, p. 873) expresses the concern as follows:

> The otherwise laudable requirement to treat others civilly may place a disproportionate burden on groups in society who have to shout or behave in ways that are deemed uncivil in order to be heard… Life in a political community, or in a public sphere more generally, brings together individuals and groups with different identities, access to power and standing in the eyes of others. By virtue of the sameness and uniformity it imposes on difference, the claim is that civility excludes or dilutes those voices already most likely to be lost in the conservation.

Critical literature on civility abounds with examples of situations in which labels and discourses of civility and incivility have been used to silence and downgrade groups within political communities (Jamieson et al. 2015; Bejan 2017; Thiranagama et al. 2018). Linda Zerrilli (2014, p. 108), for example, highlights how "throughout American history, disenfranchised minorities, such as women and African-Americans, have been regularly accused of incivility just by virtue of daring to show up in public and press their rights claims". So too, and at the same time when concerns about the political apathy of youth are high, when young people make a stand to make their interests known, such as the youth climate change strikes, they are often "readily dismissed in very public ways" (Walsh 2014). Walsh (2014) and Berents (2014) both bring our attention to responses to student protests to funding cuts to higher education in Australia, and the ways in which leading politicians and public commentators labelled the students as "selfish thugs", "bullies" and "an embarrassment". In such circumstances, to remain "civil" risks becoming unfailing civility, meaning that the domination and unjust silencing of voices must be challenged. The burden to do so rests not only with those being oppressed, but also with all citizens who see their fellows being subjugated and who share a concern for their well-being. To repeat from earlier in this book, we must be mindful that outward appearances of civility can be a façade and can hide the true motivations of those claiming to be civil. Citizens, then, must be vigilant as to when discourses of civility act in undemocratic ways.

Justified Incivility

In what remains of this chapter, some tentative thoughts are offered regarding when it is justified to be uncivil. In suggesting that incivility *can* be justified in certain situations a number of careful steps need to be taken. A first initial step, as raised above, is to recognise that political discourse can become overly constrained by norms of civility, thereby ruling out or marginalising those who do not have access to the forms of capital required for "civil" deliberation. A criticism common of advocates of deliberative democracy, for example, is that they (often by invoking Rawls' principle of public reason) sometimes expect a form of public dialogue which is too narrow and which stifles emotional displays. On this critique, deliberation rewards eloquence and restrain over passionate engagement, unfairly demeaning "on seemingly democratic grounds the views of those who are less likely to present their arguments in ways that we recognize as characteristically deliberative" (Sanders 1997, p. 349). Under these conditions, civility can serve to "de-legitimize the expression of important attitudes—such as anger and indignation—that can be *just* and *appropriate* responses to relationships, practices, and institutions that are defective from a democratic point of view" (Ward 2017, p. 118; emphasis in original).

A second step is to argue that justified incivility has to be responsive to the situation and context. Most clearly, when faced with prolonged prejudice, abuse and vitriol the justified, even moral, response will not be civility, for that would tend towards the excess of unfailing civility. As Waldron (2013, p. 4) suggests, "sometimes hostility and combativeness are what a situation requires; sometimes it is important to be rude and to act outraged…". Again, Curzer (2012, p. 88) is helpful in this regard, arguing that "uncivil actions are sometimes beneficial to those who perform them, even with respect to groups that value civility. Aristotelian civility is flexible. It allows for uncivil actions of conscious-raising and revolution". He continues: (2012, p. 89):

> I suggest that the right rule for Aristotelian civility is something like this: "Act civilly except when only uncivil action will gain a hearing from an advantaged, unpersuadable, civil group, and when doing so is worth it". A civil person is civil to people who are open-minded enough to be persuadable through civil discourse.

I find this line of argument persuasive, not least because it provides a mechanism for understanding when incivility can seek to make the interests of those most marginalised and left out of political discourse known and heard. As such, and through allowing for uncivil actions and viewing unfailing civility as a vice, the stance is able to respond to the concern that the boundaries of civility are necessarily set and controlled by those with power. Of course, no consistent conceptualisation of civility will allow for uncivil actions in all or even most circumstances—that would be to descend into the vice of incivility and will lead to democratic instability. We need, then, some additional conditions in order to guide when and what uncivil actions are the right response and to flesh out Curzer's position that uncivil actions are justified when they "will gain a hearing from an advantaged, unpersuadable, civil group, and when doing so is worth it".

Let us start with the target of uncivil responses. Any justified incivility must take as its target *those who, through misuse of their power, consistently and arbitrarily deny others a voice in the deliberative process*. In this way, justified incivility represents a response to those who fail to be civil themselves; those who fail to listen, who deny others their humanity, who hold steadfast in their views not through integrity but through dogmatism, who show no empathy for others, who descend into prejudice, vitriol and threats, and who put their narrow self-interest over those of their fellow citizens and so on. As Curzer (2012, p. 95) suggests, those misusing their power must be "shocked by uncivil consciousness-raising into giving an open-minded hearing to the grievances of the disadvantaged". Of course, in order to gain a fair hearing or to raise awareness of subjugation and denial of voice, uncivil action may—intentionally or otherwise—disrupt the lives other fellow citizens who are not immediately to blame. Nevertheless, the main target of justified incivility must be those whom are in some way deserving of the action.

Justified uncivil action must also *be proportionate*. Extensive disruption to public transport systems, for instance, may well be a relevant form of uncivil action when long-standing marginalisation and a denial of humanity is concerned, but is not proportionate for minor planning disputes. For this reason, and so the level of proportionality can be judged by fellow citizens, there is an onus on those taking uncivil action to *publicise their case*, making clear the reasons why such actions are necessary, which interests they serve and why the action is proportionate. An illustrative case is provided by the Extinction Rebellion organisation, which uses "non-violent civil disobedience in an attempt to halt mass extinction and minimise the risk of social collapse".[9] The organisation's website sets out, for example, their policy on emergency vehicles and offers a justification of the inconvenience caused to travellers and businesses affected by their action.[10] A further condition is that *uncivil action must only be approached and enacted as a means to an end and not as an end in itself*. Once a hearing is granted and it is clear that those previously denied a hearing are able to participate as equals in the deliberative process, any

---

[9] https://rebellion.earth/the-truth/about-us/

[10] https://rebellion.earth/the-truth/faqs/

uncivil actions start to lose their justification and legitimacy. In other words, justified incivility must always aim at gaining a seat at the table of political deliberation and not at coercing or denying a voice to others once that seat is gained.

Conclusion

The focus of this chapter has been the nature of civil conduct. It has been argued that civil conduct places certain general demands upon citizens, including sharing their interests and listening to those of others, shunning dogmatism, being attentive to diverse interests and enacting an engaged form of toleration. Deliberative forums are both dependent on civility and, in turn, provide a crucial forum for civility to be expressed and to flourish. It has also been suggested that the demands of civility include vigilance on the part of all citizens to identify and remedy situations in which "civility" is used to silence, subjugate and marginalise those with less power. In this chapter, and by invoking Curzer's work on civility as an intermediate mean between unfailing civility and incivility, I have also sought to tease out some of the boundaries of civility in contemporary western democracies. In doing so, I have offered some tentative thoughts as to certain conditions under which incivility may be justified in order that the interests of groups subject to persistent and arbitrary suppression and marginalisation can be publicised. In the next chapter, attention shifts to the second component of political civility set out in the introductory chapter—mutual fellow-feeling.

References

Anderson, E. (2004). The cosmopolitan canopy. *Annals of the American Academy of Political and Social Science, 595*, 14–31.

Bejan, T. M. (2017). *Mere civility: Disagreement and the limits of toleration*. Cambridge, MA: Harvard University Press.

Berents, H. (2014, June 4). 'Slackers or delinquents? No, just politically engaged youth'. *The Conversation*. Retrieved July 18, 2019, from https://theconversation.com/slackers-or-delinquents-no-just-politically-engaged-youth-27218

Boyd, R. (2006). The value of civility. *Urban Studies, 43*(5/6), 863–878.

British Broadcasting Corporation. (2019, June 20). *Biden refuses to apologise for working with racist senators*. Retrieved June 30, 2019, from https://www.bbc.co.uk/news/world-us-canada-48696126

Calhoun, C. (2000). The virtue of civility. *Philosophy & Public Affairs, 29*(3), 251–275.

Coe, K., Kenski, K., & Rains, S. A. (2014). Online and uncivil? Patterns and determinants of incivility in newspaper website comments. *Journal of Communication, 64*, 658–679.

Cohen, J. (1997). Deliberation and democratic legitimacy. In J. Bohman & W. Rehg (Eds.), *Deliberative democracy: Essays on reason and politics*. Cambridge, MA: Massachusetts Institute of Technology Press.

Cohen, J. (2012). Reflections on civility. In C. Clayton & R. Elgar (Eds.), *Civility and democracy in America: A reasonable understanding* (pp. 119–123). Pullman, WA: Washington State University Press.

Comte-Sponville, A. (2001). *A short treatise on the great virtues: The uses of philosophy in everyday life*. London: Vintage.

Curzer, H. J. (2012). An Aristotelian account of civility. In D. S. Mower & W. L. Robison (Eds.), *Civility in politics and education*. New York: Routledge.

Delgado, M. M. (2018). Civility, empathy, democracy and memory. *Performance Research: A Journal for the Performing Arts, 23*(4–5), 328–336.

Dryzek, J. S. (2010). *Foundations and frontiers of deliberative governance*. Oxford, UK: Oxford University Press.

Edyvane, D. (2017a). The passion for civility. *Political Studies Review, 15*(3), 344–354.

Edyvane, D. (2017b). Toleration and civility. *Social Theory and Practice, 43*(3), 449–471.

Elias, N. (2000). *The civilizing process: Sociogenetic and psychogenetic investigations*. Oxford, UK: Blackwell.

Eriksen, E. O. (2018). Getting to agreement: Mechanisms of deliberative decision-making. *International Theory, 10*(3), 374–408.

Farrelly, C. (2007). *Justice, democracy and reasonable agreement*. New York: Palgrave Macmillan.

Fishkin, J., & Luskin, R. (2005). Experimenting with a democratic ideal: Deliberative polling and public opinion. *Acta Politica, 40*, 284–298.

Fox, C. (2018, August 17). The dangers of illiberal liberalism. *The Economist*. https://www.economist.com/open-future/2018/08/17/the-dangers-of-illiberal-liberalism

Galarza Molina, R., & Jennings, F. J. (2018). The role of civility and metacommunication in Facebook discussions. *Communication Studies, 69*(1), 42–66.

Glendon, M. A. (1995). Forgotten questions. In M. A. Glendon (Ed.), *Seedbeds of virtue: Sources of competence, character and citizenship in American society* (pp. 1–16). Lanham, MD: Madison Books.

Gutmann, A., & Thompson, D. (1990). Moral conflict and political consensus. *Ethics, 101*(1), 64–88.

Gutmann, A., & Thompson, D. (2002). Deliberative democracy beyond process. *Journal of Political Philosophy, 10*(2), 153–174.

Gutmann, A., & Thompson, D. (2004). *Why deliberative democracy?* Princeton, NJ: Princeton University Press.

Haldane, J. (2019). Responding to discord: Why public reason is not enough. In J. Arthur (Ed.), *Virtues in the public sphere: Citizenship, civic friendship and duty* (pp. 201–212). London: Routledge.

Hume, D. (1985). In E. Miller (Ed.), *Essays: Moral, political and literary*. Carmel, IN: Liberty Fund.

Jacobs, L. R., Cook, F. L., & Delli Carpini, M. X. (2009). *Talking together: Public deliberation and political participation in America*. Chicago: University of Chicago Press.

Jamieson, K. H., Volinsky, A., Weitz, I., & Kenski, K. (2015). The political uses and abuses of civility and incivility. In K. H. Jamieson & K. Kenski (Eds.), *The oxford handbook of political communication*. Online publication.

Jeffrey, A., & Staeheli, L. A. (2015). Learning citizenship: Civility, civil society, and the possibilities of citizenship. In K. P. Kallio, S. Mills, & T. Skelton (Eds.), *Politics, citizenship and rights* (pp. 1–12). Singapore: Springer.

Kelly, T. (2018). The potential for civility: British pacifists in the second world war. *Anthropological Theory, 18*(2–3), 198–216.

Kingwell, M. (1994). *A civil tongue: Justice, dialogue, and the politics of pluralism*. University Park, PA: Pennsylvania State University Press.

Kristjánsson, K. (2006). Agreeableness. *The Journal of Value Inquiry, 40*, 33–43.

Lepp, E. (2018). Division on ice: Shared space and civility in Belfast. *Journal of Peacebuilding & Development, 13*(1), 32–45.

List, C. (2017). Deliberation and agreement. In S. W. Rosenberg (Ed.), *Deliberation, participation and democracy: Can the people govern?* (pp. 64–81). Basingstoke, UK: Palgrave Macmillan.

Mansbridge, J. (1983). *Beyond adversary democracy*. Chicago: University of Chicago Press.

Mitchell, L. (2018). Civility and collective action: Soft speech, loud roars, and the politics of recognition. *Anthropological Theory, 18*(2–3), 217–247.

Mower, D. S., & Robison, W. L. (Eds.). (2012). *Civility in politics and education.* New York: Routledge.

Nehring, H. (2011). Civility' in history: Some observations on the history of the concept. *European Review of History-Revue européenne d'histoire, 18*(3), 313–333.

Papacharissi, Z. (2004). Democracy online: Civility, politeness, and the democratic potential of online political discussion groups. *New Media & Society, 6*, 259–283.

Pettit, P. (1997). *Republicanism: A theory of freedom and government.* Oxford, UK: Oxford University Press.

Phillips, T., & Stuart, H. (2018). *An age of incivility: Understanding the new politics.* London: Policy Exchange.

Sandel, M. (1996, December 29). Making nice is not the same as doing good. *New York Times.* Retrieved May 30, 2019, from https://www.nytimes.com/1996/12/29/opinion/making-nice-is-not-the-same-as-doing-good.html

Sanders, L. (1997). Against deliberation. *Political Theory, 25*, 347–376.

Scanlon, T. M. (1996). The difficulty of tolerance. In D. Heyd (Ed.), *Toleration: An elusive virtue* (pp. 226–239). Princeton, NJ: Princeton University Press.

Scheffler, S. (2010). *Equality and tradition: Selected essays.* Oxford, UK: Oxford University Press.

Smyth, L., & McKnight, M. (2013). Maternal situations: Sectarianism and civility in a divided city. *The Sociological Review, 61*, 304–322.

Sulkin, T., & Simon, A. (2001). Habermas in the lab: A study of deliberation in an experimental setting. *Political Psychology, 22*, 809–826.

The Guardian. (2018, March 8). *How 99 strangers in a Dublin hotel broke Ireland's abortion deadlock.* https://www.theguardian.com/world/2018/mar/08/how-99-strangers-in-a-dublin-hotel-broke-irelands-abortion-deadlock

Thiranagama, S. (2018). The civility of strangers? Caste, ethnicity, and living together in postwar Jaffna, Sri Lanka. *Anthropological Theory, 18*(2–3), 357–381.

Thiranagama, S., Kelly, T., & Forment, C. (2018). Introduction: Whose civility? *Anthropological Theory, 18*(2–3), 153–174.

Waldron, J. (2013). Civility and formality. *New York University Public Law and Legal Theory Working Papers.* Paper 428. http://lsr.nellco.org/nyu_plltwp/428

Walsh, L. (2014, June 22). Our democracy is the loser when voices of youth are marginalised. *The Conversation.* Retrieved July 18, 2019, from https://theconversation.com/our-democracy-is-the-loser-when-voices-of-youth-are-marginalised-27511

Walzer, M. (1974). Civility and civic virtue in contemporary America. *Social Research, 41*(4), 593–611.

Ward, I. (2017). Democratic civility and the dangers of niceness. *Political Theology, 18*(2), 115–136.

Washington Examiner. (2019, June 19). *Harris blasts Biden for praising work with segregationalists: If they had their way, I would literally not be standing here.* https://www.washingtonexaminer.com/news/campaigns/kamala-harris-blasts-joe-biden-for-praising-work-with-segregationists-if-they-had-their-way-i-would-literally-not-be-standing-here

Young, I. M. (2000). *Inclusion and democracy.* Oxford, UK: Oxford University Press.

Zerrilli, L. (2014). Against civility: A feminist perspective. In A. Sarat (Ed.), *Civility, legality and justice in America* (pp. 107–131). Cambridge, MA: Cambridge University Press.

Zurn, C. F. (2013). Political civility: Another illusionistic ideal. *Public Affairs Quarterly, 27*(4), 341–368.

Chapter 3
Civility and Mutual Fellow-Feeling

Abstract This chapter examines the second component of political conduct intro-duced in Chap. 1—mutual fellow-feeling. Recognising the challenges of close com-munal bonds in contemporary, large, heterogeneous democracies, a case is made for conceiving the bonds between citizens in terms of an Aristotelian notion of civic friendship. The key argument of the chapter is that civility as a civic virtue for con-temporary western democracies is strengthened when we understand it in relational terms and as intimately connected with a form of partnership between citizens who share a sense of mutual positive regard. In this sense, civility describes relationships (i.e. the relationship between A and B is civil or uncivil) and is supported or limited by the nature of our relationships (i.e. the positive regard between C and D supports civil conduct between them, while the dislike or hatred between X and Y severely limits civil conduct between them). Civility operates in a fluid and dynamic way, able to rise and fall, and can therefore be understood as a precious resource which requires constant attention, cultivation and protection within democratic societies through formative processes. This latter point, it will be argued, also acts as a reminder that where democratic processes and relationships are problematic—when they are, for instance, corrupt, overly antagonistic, un-inclusive and so on—this will be to the further detriment of levels of civility.

Keywords Civility · Mutual fellow-feeling · Well-wishing · Civic friendship · Formative processes

© The Author(s), under exclusive license to Springer Nature Singapore Pte   35
Ltd. 2019
A. Peterson, *Civility and Democratic Education*, SpringerBriefs in Education,
https://doi.org/10.1007/978-981-15-1014-4_3

Introduction

In the introductory chapter of this book, two elements of political civility were identified: (1) civil conduct and (2) mutual fellow-feeling. The previous chapter concentrated on the first of these—civic conduct. The purpose of this present chapter is to attend to the second element by expanding the account of civility offered so far to explore the collective and communal basis of civility in contemporary, large, heterogeneous democracies. It will be argued that civility is strengthened by, and in turn strengthens, levels of connection between fellow citizens. The Aristotelian notion of civic friendship will be employed as a conceptual tool for examining a relationship between citizens characterised by fellow-feeling and well-wishing. The key argument of the chapter is that civility as a civic virtue for contemporary western democracies is strengthened when we understand it in relational terms and as intimately connected with a form of partnership between citizens who share a sense of mutual positive regard. In this sense, civility describes relationships (i.e. the relationship between A and B is civil or uncivil) and is supported or limited by the nature of our relationships (i.e. the positive regard between C and D supports civil conduct between them, while the dislike or hatred between X and Y severely limits civil conduct between them). Where levels of civic friendship are high, civility will be supported and where levels of civic friendship are low, incivility will increase. Civility operates in a fluid and dynamic way, able to rise and fall, and can therefore be understood as a precious resource which requires constant attention, cultivation and protection within democratic societies through formative processes. This latter point, it will be argued, also acts as a reminder that where democratic processes and relationships are problematic—when they are, for instance, corrupt, overly antagonistic, un-inclusive and so on—this will be to the further detriment of levels of civility.

My argument about the sociability needed to sustain civility is not new, and is a reasonably consistent strand of existing theorisations of civility. For example, Shils (1997, p. 340) has contended that "the individual who acts with civility regards the individuals who are its objects as being one with oneself, as being parts of a single entity", while Boyd (2006, p. 866) suggests that civility "supposes an active and positive sociability between the person who is civil and the one to whom this virtue is directed". Yet, different interpretations of the nature and depth of this positive sociability can be readily identified. According to Stephen Carter (1998, p. xii), civility involves "an attitude of respect, even love, for our fellow citizens", while, and in contrast, John Cuddihy (1978, p. 210) argued that "in a regime of civility, everybody doesn't love everybody. Everybody doesn't even respect everybody. Everybody 'shows respect for' everybody". I think the concepts of respect and love are instructive, but neither really hits the nail on the head—particularly without much more detailed explanation. Respect is certainly important, but in and of itself calls for respect run the risks of ubiquity and ambiguity. Ubiquity because the call for more respect is a frequently cited and ongoing concern in any political community. Ambiguity not just because respect is a rather general term, but because on a general understanding, and without further definition, it requires only that we take the feelings of others into account but not necessarily that we have concern for others and wish them well as common participants in a collective enterprise. Love is too strong, or at least, if love is involved it is certainly a very different form of love to that which one might ordinarily feel for one's family, or even one's personal friends. As I will suggest in what follows, civic friendships do not involve the intimacy love suggests.

There is a need, then, to be clear about what form of positive sociability is involved so far as civility is concerned. To this end, this chapter comprises two main sections. The first examines the nature of positive sociability through the prism of civic friendship and the associated concepts of mutual fellow-feeling and well-wishing. Arguing for the contemporary relevance of civic friendship and the view that such friendship holds an important relationship with civility, this first section also responds to some key challenges for civic friendship today. The second section explores those formative processes that shape, cultivate or indeed inhibit civility within the public realm. In the second section, and as set out in the introduction to this book, the public realm is understood broadly to include a wide array of democratic institutions, organisations and practises, including those of the state and wider civil society. The focus of the second section paves the way for Chap. 4, which concentrates more specifically on civility and democratic education within the education and schooling of young people.

Civic Friendship, Fellow-Feeling and Well-Wishing

In Chap. 2's discussion of tolerance, the following contention offered by Michael Walzer (1974, p. 601) was cited:

> We expect citizens to be tolerant of one another. This is probably as close as we can come to that "friendship" which Aristotle thought should characterize relations among members of the same political community. For friendship is only possible within a relatively small homogeneous city, but toleration reaches out infinitely.

In these words, Walzer alludes to a couple of important reflections, namely that when invoking Aristotle's concept of civic friendship we should remember the size of the city-states he had in mind and that the expansion of democracies in the modern period brings serious challenges for developing widespread social bonds between citizens.

Noting the challenges provided by large, heterogeneous democracies for the development of civic virtues, the aim in this section is to suggest that civic friendship, of a particular type, *is* possible in contemporary democracies and, moreover, that civility holds an important relationship with civic friendship. While I suggest that the two concepts are intimately connected, civility and civic friendship are not direct synonyms. The social bonds of civic friendship provide a foundation for civility, bringing citizens together and aiding the stability of democratic political communities. Where social bonds are weak, the commitment to civility is likely to be low. In turn, the engagements and connections made possible by civility further build the bond between citizens. At least, that is what I will argue in what follows.

Focusing on the social bonds of civic friendship is to argue that for civility to flourish, citizens need care about each other and be concerned about certain interests, actions and experiences of their fellow citizens. In other words, a fundamental way civic friendship can be recognised and performed in contemporary democracies is *through* civility. This does not require that citizens necessarily care about *all* interests, actions and experiences of others within their political communities. Clearly, whether a fellow citizen prefers blue cars or red cars or prefers to live in a city or a village is largely, if not wholly, immaterial so far as the health of the democratic community is concerned. Neither does this expectation of care require citizens to care about *each and every* citizen on a personal level—that is clearly impossible. Rather, care and concern operate on a general level in the sense that citizens do (or should!) care about the interests, actions and experiences of other citizens and that citizens do (or should!) exhibit concern when the interests of given groups and fellow citizens are marginalised or dominated unfairly (Schwarzenbach 1996).

In suggesting that civility is best understood as involving a bond between fellow citizens I seek to counter the view that civility is "a cold virtue not a warm one, not really a matter of affection or benevolence" (Waldron 2013, p. 4). At a general level, we can see the importance of human connection when we consider certain situations in which civility is absent. As Richard Boyd (2006, p. 873; emphasis added) argues:

> To fail to be civil to someone-to treat them harshly, rudely or condescendingly-is not only to be guilty of bad manners. It also and more ominously *signals disdain or contempt for them as moral beings.*

It is precisely this disdain that is so often characteristic of uncivil political discourse today. Those with alternative views on key matters—Trump's Presidency, the UK's leaving the European Union and so on—are often treated not only as holding different views, but also as being morally inferior and morally contemptible. When citizens care for their fellow citizens, understanding citizenship as a partnership, they listen to the views of fellow citizens and are open-minded to these views, signalling a recognition of their fellow citizens as equal moral beings and as co-participants in the democratic project. When they do so, citizens act, that is, as civic friends.

Civic Friendship

To understand Aristotle's concept of civic friendship requires that we engage with various aspects of his works—the *Nicomachean Ethics* (2009), the *Eudemian Ethics* (2011), *The Art of Rhetoric* and the *Politics* (1992)—as well as with contemporary commentaries on civic friendship. Before progressing to what is meant specifically by *civic* friendship, we need to understand Aristotle's wider conception of friendship, or *philia*. Aristotle understands *philia* in this general sense as "doing well by someone for his own sake, out of concern for *him*, and not, or not merely, out of concern for oneself"—(Cooper 1990, p. 302). In Book 2, Chap. 4 of *The Art of Rhetoric*, Aristotle (1991, p. 89) contends that "your friend is the sort of man who shares your pleasure in what is good and your pain in what is unpleasant, for your sake and for no other reason". Aristotle distinguishes between three types of friendships—those based on pleasure, those based on character and virtue, and those based on utility.

While others offer different readings,[1] following scholars such as Cooper (1990, 1999), Schwarzenbach (1996) and Leontsini (2013), I understand civic friendship as a form of friendship based on utility and common advantage, but which also includes the mutual well-wishing for each other's sake of Aristotle's general sense of friendship. Aristotle suggests that "civic friendship, more than any other, is based on utility, for it is the lack of self-sufficiency that brings people together" (EE 1242a6-9). In addition, Aristotle seems to reserve friendships based on character and virtue for closer, more intimate relationships and to limit the extent of these:

> Those who have many friends and mix intimately with them all are thought to be no one's friend, except in the way proper to fellow citizens, and such people are also called obsequious. In the way proper to fellow citizens, indeed, it is possible to be the friend of man yet not be obsequious but a genuinely good man; but one cannot have with many people the friendship based on virtue and the character of our friends themselves, and we must be content if we find even a few such. (NE 1171a16-20).

Civic friendship is not of this intimate kind, and operates on a more general level, though civic friends do care about the "kinds of persons" their fellow citizens are, care about their well-being as fellow citizens and are therefore committed to enquire and learn about the interests of fellow citizens (Schwarzenbach 1996, 2015). Partly for this reason, civic friendship is undermined when political associations are dominated by narrow interests and factionalism (Mayhew 1996).

Civic friendship exhibits a close connection with concord, or the condition of agreement within the political community. According to Aristotle concord is "not identity of opinion… nor do we say that people who have the same views on any and every subject are in accord…, but we do say that a city is in accord when men have the same opinion about what is to their interest, and choose the same actions, and do what they have resolved in common" (NE 1167a22-29). In this sense, concord is not about homogeneity, though of course the context Aristotle had in mind was much less heterogeneous than democracies today. Scorza (2004, p. 90) describes the process as one in which "friends try to govern their disagreements in such a way as to preserve and develop, rather than terminate, the bond between them". Because of the nature of political life, developing and sustaining civic friendship is challenging and requires commitment. Yack (1993, p. 125) contrasts civic friends with travellers "in the same boat":

---

[1] See, for example, Price (1989) and Curren (2019).

Because the goals of political action are not nearly as clear as the destination of a ship, the sense of sharing obstacles and dangers is not as certain to develop among citizens as it is among fellow travellers. Moreover, because these goals, unlike fellow travellers' destination, are always in the distance, this sense often dies as the result of resentment and disappointment. Nevertheless, however fragile it may be, participation in political community, Aristotle would argue, does dispose us to developing a fairly extensive and powerful sense of mutual concern.

Civic friendship is dependent upon a level of material equality between citizens (Curren 2019). Indeed, for Aristotle, civic friendship in a sense involves justice: "when men are friends they have no need for justice, while when they are just they need friendship as well, and the truest form of justice is thought to be a friendly quality" (NE 1155a26-29). In fact, in the *Eudemian Ethics* Aristotle suggests that civic friendships "are the only ones that are not merely friendships, but *partnerships* between friends... The justice on which a friendship of utility is based is justice par excellence, because it is civic justice" (EE 1242a10-14; emphasis added). The terminology of partnership is instructive, and speaks to the mutual connection and fellow-feeling between citizens. Members of a partnership look out for the interests of others, working on the basis of mutual trust and concern. So too, members of a partnership are aware that their own immediate interests may have to take second place to those of the collective. They do so not because they meekly allow their interests to be subjugated, but because they trust that fair and inclusive processes have been followed in which all voices have been paid due attention and because they perceive that their fellow citizens share this mutual trust and well-wishing (Fiala 2013).

If we understand civic friendship in this way, we can see that civility is a core way through which the fellow-feeling and well-wishing of civic friendship is embodied and enacted.[2] In this vein, in their empirical study of public deliberation in the USA, Jacobs et al. (2009, p. 117; emphasis added) draw attention to the role that deliberative political arrangements might play in this regard, arguing that:

The political and civic effects of deliberation have important implications. First, they boost engagement in forms of participation that commentators have bemoaned as declining in public life... Moreover, they provide some grounds for optimism regarding deliberation's impact on areas that we were unable to examine-notably, *the formation of the discourses and socially shared meanings that underpin civil society and democratic government.*

My argument to this point has been that through civil conduct citizens make clear their interests, identify areas of conflict and seek, via deliberative means, ways to accommodate disagreements and that doing so is made possible by, and further

---

[2] In his commentary on Aristotle, Kekes (1984, p. 434; emphasis added) refers to "civic-friendship *or* civility" rather than civic friendship *and* civility. Curzer (2012b, p. 192) offers the following way of conceiving the relationship between friendship and civility: "people with the virtue of friendliness, people who feel friendly feelings and who are disposed to accept, praise, oppose, and criticize words and deeds rightly in each situation, also have the disposition to speak and act rightly in the social sphere... Aristotle should have combined the virtue of friendliness with the disposition to speak and act rightly in the social sphere to form a single virtue that might, perhaps, be called the virtue of civility".

extends, fellow-feeling and well-wishing between citizens. Critics may respond, however, that the form of mutual association I have in mind is unlikely to be suitable or even viable in contemporary democracies. As we have seen with Walzer's contention cited above, for some, contemporary democracies are simply too large to make possible the sort of civic friendship set out above. Clearly, both the extent and nature of civic friendship are challenged by the size and plurality of contemporary representative democracies. Rather than ruling out the possibility of civic friendship, however, I would like to suggest that the challenge of size and plurality can be overcome and is not necessarily fatal.

Primarily, we should remember that civic friendships are of a general nature, much less intimate than the close, personal relationships typically used to denote friendship (Mayhew 1996; Schwarzenbach 1996). To be applicable to large societies, civic friendship, and the civility that builds from and sustains it, therefore has to incorporate an acceptance that citizens possess a relationship with others with whom they will never come in to contact. Civic friends commit—whether specifically or more generally—to working *with* and *for* others within their political communities and to do so with civility; civic friends "expect others to treat them similarly" (Kekes 1984, p. 431). In this way, while some encounters of civic friendship will be close and involved (in local neighbourhood associations, in citizen assemblies and so on), in the main civic friendship will operate at a more impersonal and removed level. For this reason, the reciprocity involved in civility as an expression of civic friendship operates on the basis that "individual acts of civic-friendship create a fund of good will upon which depositors can draw. Just as they are benevolent to strangers and passing acquaintances recognized to be fellow citizens, so they count on being benevolently treated by other citizens" (Kekes 1984, p. 431). It is unlikely that this recognition of the connection between civility and civic friendship, and in particular the way that the former expresses and sustains the latter, is always—or even often—in the minds of citizens as they go about their public lives. Nevertheless, and particularly in diverse societies that cannot rely on homogeneous interests as a foundation for political cooperation and stability, it is shared participation in the public and civic life of communities that is both the target and source of citizens' cooperative endeavour. As Shils (1997, pp. 13–14) puts it, this means conceiving other members of the political community as "fellow-citizens of equal dignity in their rights and obligations as members of civil society; it means regarding other persons, including one's adversaries, as members of the same inclusive collectivity, i.e., as members of the same society, even though they belong to different parties or to different religious communities or to different ethnic groups".

From this perspective, accepting that other citizens are different and hold different interests does not, in and of itself, endanger fellow-feeling and well-wishing. In contrast, when citizens conceive of and treat others as being of less moral worth, as being less deserving of a voice, and thus exclude them from the civic partnership, levels of civility and civic friendship suffer. Here, the words of Bhikhu Parekh (2008, p. 47) are relevant:

Members of a political community are bound to each other by countless ties. They have a common interest in maintaining a stable community, a system of basic rights and liberties, and a general climate of civility and mutual trust… They see it as their community, feel responsible for it, take an active interest in its affairs, and feel proud or ashamed when it does or does not live up to their moral expectations of it. Through all this, relations between citizens are a form of special relations.

Conceiving other members of the political community in this way involves, furthermore, that citizens practice trust and goodwill in their democratic encounters, approaching each other—at least until there is compelling evidence to the contrary—on the mutual understanding that participants are, for example, offering their viewpoints, interests and arguments in good faith. Trust and goodwill are vital for democratic collaboration (D'Olimpio 2018), and where levels of trust and goodwill are high, civility is more likely to follow.[3] Kekes (1984, p. 442) puts this in the following way:

A civil person extends his good will to all his fellow citizens without discrimination. He expects that they will treat him in as friendly and helpful manner as he treats them. In good societies, this expectation is satisfied; in bad societies, it is not. What underlies this expectation is the tacit assumption that not rights, but good will guide the conduct of fellow citizens.

The focus here on goodwill, fellow-feeling and cooperation also serves as a further reminder that, without this underpinning commitment to fellow citizens, civil behaviour can serve to mask true motivations. This point is made eloquently by Calhoun (2000, p. 261) who reminds us of the importance of civil actions being accompanied by the "civil display of the corresponding moral attitudes". Without the corresponding moral attitude, it would seem, actions with only the semblance of civility deny the inherent dignity of others as persons in their own rights, failing to view and treat them as legitimate fellow members of a shared political community.

When we consider claims that civility is in decline today it is not only the tone of political discourse that is identified as having deteriorated, but also levels of trust. Without sufficient levels of trust between citizens, political discourse is less likely to be based on the assumption that views are offered and received in good faith. Waldron (2013, p. 16) argues that "civility's first impulse is to accept the opposing view for what it is: simply a different position on a problem on which people in good faith may be opposed". Here, he draws on Rawls' (1993, p. 58) contention that "it is unrealistic to suppose that all our differences are rooted solely in ignorance and perversity, or else in the rivalries for power, status, or economic gain". The nature of political trust is, of course, complex and much existing research focuses on levels of trust between the citizen and offices and institutions of government (for an overview of existing literature, see van der Meer 2017). But, trust within political communities is not just vertical. Trust applies equally to the horizontal relationships between citizens. In fact, social trust is a condition for political trust (Zmerli and Newton 2008). Trust, though, is a precarious and risky commodity, asking those

---

[3] Some empirical studies also suggest that incivility in political discourse diminishes trust in government (Sydnor 2019; Mutz 2007; Mutz and Reeves 2005).

who invest their trust in others to open themselves with the hope that others will not abuse this trust. Recognising this point does not mean that citizens are or should be ignorant of manipulations by those with power, nor that they should overlook these when they do occur, but it does mean that citizens should be vigilant that being over-attentive to such manipulations can easily collapse into unhealthy scepticism, suspicion and cynicism. The dangers of misguided cynicism are eloquently and forcefully put by Kronman (1996, p. 731), who writes:

> It is now often said that appeals to the public interest are always and only disguised efforts to advance the private good of the person making the appeal. The modern "masters" of suspicion… have taught us to regard the seemingly selfless judgements of those who claim to have only their community's welfare at heart as a subtle ideological trick designed to advance the interests of their economic class;… Today when we hear someone invoke the public good, our first reaction is often to ask what private interest this masks, and to search for the real motive of the statement, below the surface of expression, in some other and more self-centred concern. The depths having been revealed to us, we now find it more difficult to take the surface seriously, to credit at face value the claim that one is acting for the sake of the public good and not out of private interest instead. Suspicious as we are, this claim has become for us quite literally incredible…

Closely connected to the importance for civility of trust is the importance of citizens showing patience and being able to distinguish between errors and mistakes made in good faith, and those generated from more sinister, and socially harmful, motives. When fellow citizens make errors and misjudgements in their interactions, patience is needed to tease out why these occurred and how they can be redressed, requiring that citizens approach their democratic encounters with open-mindedness and humility. As Curzer (2012a, p. 86) suggests, "we need to be praised (blamed) for our right (wrong) actions in order to keep us on track and motivated. Moreover, we need to engage in frequent dialogue about moral issues so that we can improve our moral reasoning and beliefs". When the wrongdoing is part of a wider, sustained pattern of unjustified incivility (it unfairly dominates the interests of disadvantaged groups, seeks to attain the advantage of those in power over other sections of the political community, excludes particular voices from dialogue, etc.) patience is unlikely to be appropriate. However, when *genuine* errors in discourse are treated punitively and those making the errors are cut out of further engagement they are denied their fellow membership of the political community. Just as personal friends often recognise that mistakes may be made and so offer patience and forgiveness, so too patience and forgiveness may well play an important role in sustaining fellow-feeling.

Formative Processes

A key part of the argument put forward in the last section was that civility is supported by civic friendship (civility will be in greater supply when citizens view themselves as civic friends) and that civic friendship is sustained by civility (civic friendship is made easier and is more likely to flourish when citizens are civil). In this section, I focus specifically on the idea that it makes sense to talk of cultures of civility and incivility. Cultures of civility and incivility play a formative role, and occur and operate through the workings and practices of the range of democratic institutions, processes and associations experienced by citizens. To put the claim simply, when the wider democratic culture is characterised by civility further civility is likely to result, and when it is characterised by incivility this will lead to greater incivility. The next chapter focuses on the formative role of education and schooling in cultivating civility. In this final section of this chapter, my focus is on formative processes outside of formal education and schooling that serve to cultivate civility and incivility.

While Macedo et al. (2005, p. 6) warned that "modern political scientists and those engaged in crafting public policy too often neglect the formative dimension of politics as a whole", a number of political theorists and scientists have pointed to the educational function of the institutions, norms and practices of democratic citizenship. Michael Sandel (1996, p. 321), for example, has suggested that political institutions can act as "agencies of civic education" that "inculcate the habit of attending to public things". Along comparable lines, Jochum et al. (2005, p. 10) argue that participation in civil society is "valuable because it frequently stimulates or reinforces" democratic, political engagement. In his theory of strong democracy, Benjamin Barber (1984, p. 265) argued that "[T]he taste for participation is whetted by participation: democracy breeds democracy", while Adrian Oldfield (1990, p. 155) adopted a similar tack, contending that:

> Not only is the process educative in itself—the more one participates, the more one develops the attitudes appropriate to a citizen... the example set by the initial participators will draw ever-widening groups of individuals into the political arena.

Like other civic virtues, civility, and indeed civic friendship, requires cultivation within and through political communities, including "*via* a society's constitution, its public set of laws, it major institutions and social customs" (Schwarzenbach 2015, p. 11; see also Sullivan 1995). If they are to cultivate the attentiveness, responsiveness and reflexivity in citizens needed for civility, democratic institutions and processes need to be attentive, responsive and reflexive themselves. Institutions are democratically attentive, responsive and reflexive not just when they are built on engaged participation and deliberative structures, but when they follow processes that enable decisions arrived at to be understood as provisional and open to further revision in light, for example, of new ideas or changes in circumstances (Barber 1999; Pettit 1997).

Does it, therefore, make sense to talk about cultures of civility and incivility? I suggest it does, and for a variety of reasons. First, let us consider the following. John and Joan meet at the first in a series of public meetings about the building of a large residential estate on open space adjacent to a small village. John supports the new residential estate on the basis that the local area needs more housing and with the hope that the plans will include some affordable housing for members of the local community who have increasingly been priced out of the local housing market. Joan opposes the new estate owing to her concerns that insufficient infrastructure is in place to support the expansion and about the impact on the local environment. At the first meeting, John and Joan engage in discussion, both making their views and interests known and doing so in a way which exhibits common decency and respect for the other. Indeed, the conduct of the whole meeting is positive and respectful. Arriving at the second meeting John and Joan are in a positive frame of mind. They know that they will engage with others with whom they disagree, but they have the expectation—shaped by the conduct of the first meeting—that views will be exchanged and explored in a conducive and positive way. By the third meeting in the series, John and Joan hold largely positive and proactive views about the meetings.

Now let us consider the first meeting again, but this time John and Joan conduct themselves in uncivil ways. John launches a personal attack on Joan, to which Joan responds with rudeness. The whole meeting is dominated by name-calling, shouting and personal insults, and John and Joan accuse each other of masking their true intentions. They both enter the second meeting in a very different frame of mind to our first example, and once again the meeting—and John and Joan's interactions—remain uncivil, discourteous and rude. By the third meeting in the series, John and Joan are feeling less inclined and positive about the meetings, shaped as they are by uncivil discourse.

These are simple examples, but they remind us that when deliberations are entered into with trust, good faith and a commitment to partnership civility is more likely flourish, whereas when deliberations are entered into with a lack of trust, with cynicism and on the basis of deep-rooted factionalism incivility is likely to flourish. To turn to a real example, debates about the UK's departure from the European Union are roundly identified to have become beset by a culture of incivility. Following his resignation as a government minister and his commencement of a "walk in search of common ground", Lord Bates (2019) described the prevailing culture as follows:

> In recent months it has become clear to me that the greatest problem facing this country is not how and when we leave the European Union, but rather how we heal the divisions which have opened up as a result of that process… There is an aggressiveness, intolerance and incivility which has emerged in our public discourse which is doing our country immense long-term harm. Brexit has become for us a kind of toxic court room divorce battle in which the hatred of the parents for each other, and their refusal to concede ground to the other, has all but obscured their shared love and responsibility for their children. It is time to seek selfless solutions that put the happiness and well being of all people first.

Few would deny that the culture of debate surrounding whether the UK should leave or remain members of the European Union has become toxic, shaped as it is by a profound sense of anger at, often stereotyped, positions ascribed by remainers and leavers to each other. Few would also deny that the divisions have seriously damaged the sense of partnership and mutual well-wishing between citizens across the political spectrum. A particular culture has been created in which anger and incivility dominate and which serves to fuel further incivility. I would suggest, then, that prevailing cultures of civility and incivility play an integral role in whether further responses are, themselves, civil or uncivil and that for this reason it makes sense to talk about spirals of civility and incivility, and to understand that where civility is in abundance (i.e. there is a culture of civility), further civility will be encouraged and cultivated and will spiral upwards. In contrast, where incivility is rife (i.e. there is a culture of incivility) further incivility will manifest and civility will spiral downwards.

It would also be remiss not to consider briefly what some viewpoints on newer forms of political dialogue suggest about cultures and norms of civility and incivility. Here, I think there are a few tentative, yet notable, points to highlight, each of which is in need of further theorisation and empirical examination. First, various studies suggest that it is the case that those engaging in online political discussions take a cue from the preceding or general tone of the conduct so far. Where the general tone is civil, participants adopt the civil mode in further posts. In their empirical study examining the impact of modelling on online political discussions, Han et al. (2018, p. 7) found that participants involved in civil discussions "followed the mode of civility, were less likely to go off topic, and were more likely to offer a fresh perspective to the discussion". Similarly, in a study on Facebook discussions, Galarza Molina and Jennings (2018, p. 57) found "two normatively desirable benefits to civil discussion: more engagement and more civil comments".

Second, there seems to be some differences across studies regarding whether similar processes are at play where discussions are uncivil. In their study focusing on the use of insulting language and messages in online political discussions—what they term "flaming"—Hmielowski et al. (2014, p. 1206–1207) report that "the prevalence of flaming in online contexts… may lead to people to see aggressive behaviors as acceptable". Similarly, Sobieraj and Berry (2011) have written about the increasing prevalence of political discourse in blogs, talk radio and cable news programmes in the USA that has have moved from incivility in general terms towards outrage (both its expression and generation). Both of these studies would seem to suggest a downward spiral of civility when cultures of incivility are dominant. A different reading is provided, however, by Han et al.'s (2018) research. They found that it was *not* the case that participants followed the mode of incivility. Instead, these participants either shifted to engage in "metacommunication, voicing their frustrations and calling for a more civil conversation", or just checked out from the discussion altogether. In another study, Galarza Molina and Jennings (2018, p. 56) found that while metacommunication about civility did not significantly affect levels of civility, metacommunication did provide a model through which others engaged in further metacommunication. Research from Han and Brazeal (2015) and Chen and Lu (2017) reports that civil discourse, but not uncivil discourse, motivated those involved towards further political participation in that mode. These studies, at least in online spaces, point to a range of options and behaviours that are available to citizens when incivility is encountered, which include remaining civil, challenging incivility directly, challenging incivility indirectly through metacommunication and detaching from the discussion altogether.

Third, discussing incivility in political discourse Jonathan Haidt (APA 2018) has suggested that the proliferation of forms of communication is fundamentally changing the wider norms of social and political conversation in ways that transcend across various forms of democratic encounters:

> This is what really scares me… a civil society needs lots of different zones where different practices and norms take place. What we do in the public square when we yell at each other has to be different from what we do in the classroom, which has to be different from what we do in the doctor's office or the courtroom or anywhere else… Social media has knocked down all the walls, it's all the same everywhere… Everything is politics all the time.

Haidt's assertion is that the ways that some citizens communicate on social media are now being employed in other aspects of citizens' lives. In other words, citizens who are happy to tweet abusive messages at their political opponents are increasingly happy to shout abuse at them in the streets or as they go about their private lives. This shift Haidt identifies towards a knocking down of the walls between different zones of social and political interactions, if indeed it is real, suggests that cultures of incivility may be pervasive across spheres of democratic life. It also raises serious questions regarding the sort of cultures and behaviours young citizens are being educated into. If children and young people experience incivility as a common part of their daily experiences, and see their role models acting in uncivil ways, it would not be surprising that they would imitate and follow such patterns of behaviour. This is just one reason why the educational task of cultivating civility—a task that must pay due attention to prevailing cultures—is such an essential and pressing part of democratic education.

Conclusion

Complementing the view expounded in Chap. 2 that political civility involves civic conduct, this chapter has argued that political civility is intimately connected to a widespread sense of mutual fellow-feeling between citizens. The Aristotelian idea of civic friendship offers some conceptual detail for conceiving that fellow-feeling, understanding positive sociability between citizens to be founded on a commitment to working in partnership and reciprocal well-wishing. This requires of citizens that their words and actions convey their civic friendship to their fellow citizens, both specifically and generally. In addition, it has been suggested that the cultures and operations of democratic institutions, organisations and processes play a crucial formative role in developing and inhibiting civility and incivility. Levels of civility and incivility do not exist independently from prevailing cultures and practises within political communities. Where relationships between citizens recognise common humanity, share mutual concern and understand citizenship as a partnership, civility will flourish and, in turn, will provide a mechanism to strengthen civic bonds. Where relationships are characterised by injustice, denial of human dignity and the prioritisation of factional interests, civility will suffer and incivility will grow. Civility needs, then, a fertile and supportive environment if it is to flourish.

And so, in the next chapter, discussion moves to focus more specifically on cultivating civility within and through democratic education and schooling.

References

American Psychological Association. (2018, October 5). *Panel discusses nation's decline in civil discourse.* Retrieved June 20, 2019, from https://www.apa.org/members/content/civil-discourse

Aristotle. (1991). *The art of rhetoric* (H. C. Lawson-Trancred, Trans.). London: Penguin.

Aristotle. (1992). In T. J. Saunders (Ed.), *The politics.* London: Penguin.

Aristotle. (2009). *The Nicomachean ethics.* Oxford, UK: Oxford University Press.

Aristotle. (2011). *The Eudemian ethics.* Oxford, UK: Oxford University Press.

Barber, B. (1984). *Strong democracy: Participatory politics for a new age.* Berkeley, CA: University of California Press.

Barber, B. (1999). The discourse of civility. In S. L. Elkin & K. E. Soltan (Eds.), *Citizen competence and democratic institutions.* Pennsylvania State University Press: University Park, PA.

Bates, L. (2019, April 24). Brexit's court room battle has become toxic – I'm quitting as a minister to search for common ground. *Politics Home.* https://www.politicshome.com/news/uk/political-parties/conservative-party/opinion/house-lords/103407/lord-bates-brexits-court

Boyd, R. (2006). The value of civility. *Urban Studies, 43*(5/6), 863–878.

Calhoun, C. (2000). The virtue of civility. *Philosophy & Public Affairs, 29*(3), 251–275.

Carter, S. L. (1998). *Civility: Manners, morals and the etiquette of democracy.* New York, NY: Basic Books.

Chen, G., & Lu, S. (2017). Online political discourse: Exploring differences in effects of civil and uncivil disagreement in news website comments. *Journal of Broadcasting & Electronic Media, 61*(1), 108–125.

Cooper, J. (1990). Aristotle on friendship. In A. O. Rorty (Ed.), *Essays on Aristotle's ethics* (pp. 301–340). Berkeley, CA: University of California Press.

Cooper, J. (1999). Political animals and civic friendship. In J. Cooper (Ed.), *Reason and emotion* (pp. 356–377). Princeton, NJ: Princeton University Press.

Cuddihy, J. (1978). *The ordeal of civility: Freud, Marx, Lévi-Strauss, and the Jewish struggle with modernity.* New York: Basic Books.

Curren, R. (2019). Populism and the fate of civic friendship. In J. Arthur (Ed.), *Virtues in the public sphere: Citizenship, civic friendship and duty* (pp. 92–107). London: Routledge.

Curzer, H. J. (2012a). An Aristotelian account of civility. In D. S. Mower & W. L. Robison (Eds.), *Civility in politics and education.* New York: Routledge.

Curzer, H. J. (2012b). *Aristotle and the virtues.* Oxford, UK: Oxford University Press.

D'Olimpio, L. (2018). Trust as a virtue in education. *Educational Philosophy and Theory, 50*(2), 193–202.

Fiala, A. (2013). The fragility of civility: Virtue, civil society, and tragic breakdowns of civility. *Dialogue and Universalism, 3,* 109–122.

Galarza Molina, R., & Jennings, F. J. (2018). The role of civility and metacommunication in Facebook discussions. *Communication Studies, 69*(1), 42–66.

Han, S.-H., & Brazeal, L. M. (2015). Playing nice: Modelling civility in online political discussions. *Communication Research Reports, 32*(1), 20–28.

Han, S.-H., Brazeal, L. M., & Pennington, N. (2018). Is civility contagious? Examining the impact of modelling in online political discussions. *Social Media + Society, 4*(3), 1–12.

Hmielowski, J. D., Hutchens, M. J., & Cicchirillo, V. J. (2014). Living in an age of online incivility: Examining the conditional indirect effects of online discussion on political flaming. *Information, Communication & Society, 17*(10), 1196–1211.

Jacobs, L. R., Cook, F. L., & Delli Carpini, M. X. (2009). *Talking together: Public deliberation and political participation in America*. Chicago: University of Chicago Press.

Jochum, V., Pratten, B., & Wilding, K. (2005). *Civil renewal and active citizenship: a guide to the debate*. Retrieved June 20, 2019, from https://www.ncvo.org.uk/images/documents/policy_and_research/participation/civil_renewal_active_citizenship.pdf

Kekes, J. (1984). Civility and society. *History of Philosophy Quarterly, 1*(4), 429–443.

Kronman, A. T. (1996). Civility. *Faculty Scholarship Series, 1055*. https://digitalcommons.law.yale.edu/fss_papers/1055.

Leontsini, E. (2013). The motive of society: Aristotle on civic friendship, justice, and concord. *Res Publica, 19*, 21–35.

Macedo, S., Alex-Assensoh, Y., Berry, J. M., Brintnall, M., Campbell, D. E., Fraga, L. R., et al. (2005). *Democracy at risk: How political choices undermine citizen participation, and what we can do about it*. Washington, DC: Brookings Institution Press.

Mayhew, R. (1996). *Aristotle on civic friendship* (p. 197). The Society for Ancient Greek Philosophy Newsletter. http://orb.binghampton/sagep/197

Mutz, D. (2007). Effects of 'in-your-face' television discourse on perceptions of a legitimate opposition. *American Political Science Review, 101*(4), 621–645.

Mutz, D. C., & Reeves, B. (2005). The new videomalaise: Effects of televised incivility on political trust. *American Political Science Review, 99*(1), 1–15.

Oldfield, A. (1990). *Citizenship and community, civil republicanism and the modern state*. London: Routledge.

Parekh, B. (2008). *A new politics of identity: Political principles for an interdependent world*. Basingstoke, UK: Palgrave Macmillan.

Pettit, P. (1997). *Republicanism: A theory of freedom and government*. Oxford, UK: Oxford University Press.

Price, A. W. (1989). *Love and friendship in plato and aristotle*. Oxford: Oxford University Press.

Rawls, J. (1993). *Political liberalism*. New York: Columbia University Press.

Sandel, M. (1996). *Democracy's discontent: America in search of a public philosophy*. London: Belknap Harvard.

Schwarzenbach, S. A. (1996). On civic friendship. *Ethics, 107*(1), 97–128.

Schwarzenbach, S. A. (2015). Fraternity, solidarity and friendship. *AMITY: The Journal of Friendship Studies, 3*(1), 3–18.

Scorza, J. (2004). Liberal citizenship and civic friendship. *Political Theory, 32*(1), 85–108.

Shils, E. (1997) The virtue of civility: Selected essays on liberalism, tradition, and civil society. Ed. by S. Grosby. Carmel, IN: Liberty Fund.

Sobieraj, S., & Berry, J. M. (2011). From incivility to outrage: Political discourse in blogs, talk radio, and cable news. *Political Communication, 28*(1), 19–41.

Sullivan, W. M. (1995). Reinstitutionalizing virtue in civil society. In M. A. Glendon (Ed.), *Seedbeds of virtue: Sources of competence, character and citizenship in American society* (pp. 185–200). Lanham, MD: Madison Books.

Sydnor, E. (2019). Signaling incivility: The role of speaker, substance, and tone. In R. G. Boatright, T. J. Shaffer, S. Sobieraj, & D. Goldthwaite Young (Eds.), *A crisis of civility? Political discourse and its discontents* (pp. 61–80). New York: Routledge.

van der Meer, T. W. G. (2017). Political trust and the "crisis of democracy". In *Oxford Research Encyclopedia, Politics* (pp. 1–22). Oxford, UK: Oxford University Press. https://doi.org/10.1093/acrefore/9780190228637.013.77.

Waldron, J. (2013). Civility and formality. *New York University public law and legal theory working papers*. Paper 428. http://lsr.nellco.org/nyu_plltwp/428

Walzer, M. (1974). Civility and civic virtue in contemporary America. *Social Research, 41*(4), 593–611.

Yack, B. (1993). *The problems of a political animal*. Berkeley, CA: University of California Press.

Zmerli, S., & Newton, K. (2008). Social trust and attitudes toward democracy. *The Public Opinion Quarterly, 72*(4), 706–724.

Chapter 4
Educating Civility in Schools

Abstract Drawing on the analysis of the preceding chapters, this chapter examines civility as a core component of democratic education. Focusing specifically on schools, the analysis considers educating for civility as comprising three interconnected strands: *Situating civility*—examines the importance of pupils' learning about the meanings and interpretations of civility as a prerequisite for understanding and enacting civility; *Experiencing civility*—concentrates on the educational importance of providing experiential opportunities within schools for pupils to practice civility and to reflect on these practises; *Enacting civility*—adopts a wider scope in focusing on pupil's experiences and expression of civility across their lives in schools, including the continued challenges involved. In exploring each of these strands, key opportunities and challenges for educators are highlighted and considered.

Keywords Educating civility · Situating civility · Experiencing civility · Enacting civility · Character education · Citizenship education

Introduction

Based on and extending the analysis offered so far, this final chapter takes as its focus educating for civility in schools. The decision to concentrate precisely on schools is important. Even if the school is not the *primary* moral, social and political influence in the life of a child, schools and teachers do play a key formative role in cultivating democratic virtues, often working together (and at times against) other influences such as families, peer groups and the media to produce certain kinds of people. Education and schooling are essentially moral and political matters, and the question is not whether schools play a role in shaping children's sociability but what

A. Peterson, *Civility and Democratic Education*, SpringerBriefs in Education, https://doi.org/10.1007/978-981-15-1014-4_4

this role consists of and how the role is fulfilled. Indeed, the general aim of cultivating responsible, informed and active citizens is widespread if not universal across education and schooling systems in western democracies. Yet, we must be mindful too that the trajectory of educational policy in western democracies over the last four decades has been driven largely by forces of marketisation and individualisation and that this has acted to constrain the democratic work of schools. This reminds us, moreover, that civility in schools does not happen in a vacuum and that educative processes concerning civility connect with and are shaped by wider social and political agendas and cultures.

The chapter comprises three main sections.[1] The first section—*Situating civility*—examines the importance of pupils' learning about the meanings and interpretations of civility as a prerequisite for understanding and enacting civility. The second section—*Experiencing civility*—concentrates on the educational importance of providing experiential opportunities within schools for pupils to practice civility and to reflect on these practises. The third section—*Enacting civility*—adopts a wider scope in focusing on pupil's experiences and expression of civility across their lives in schools, including the continued challenges involved.

Before proceeding to the main analysis, a number of important qualifications about terminology need to be attended to from the outset for reasons of clarity. First, a brief, working definition of democratic education is required. Democratic education as used in this chapter refers to the conscious goal of cultivating the knowledge, skills, understandings and dispositions necessary for active, informed and responsible democratic citizenship. Informed by this goal, democratic education carries with it the supposition that a large proportion of democratic education should occur in democratic forms and spaces. For this reason, democratic education cannot be equated solely with specific curricular subjects, such as the National Curriculum for Citizenship education in England or the Australian Curriculum: Civics and Citizenship in Australia (though curricular subjects clearly play a part). While various curricular for civics and citizenship education have—either explicitly or implicitly in terms of general rules, norms or dispositions to guide conduct—included a focus on civility (see, for example, Quigley and Buchanan 1991; QCA 2007; ACARA 2018), cultivating democratic citizens who are active, informed and responsible and who express democratic virtues involves much broader processes than single curricular subjects can achieve alone. Democratic education requires the cultivation of requisite knowledge, skills and emotions across the breadth of children's experiences in schools (Mander 2014). It is useful, therefore, to conceive democratic education in schools, as with character education, as involving processes that are taught, caught and sought (Jubilee Centre 2017). Second, and following from this, weaving throughout the chapter is an underlying argument that democratic education is precisely democratic when it is shaped by deliberative processes through which a range of voices, including those of pupils, are given appropriate

---

[1] The three sections of this chapter—situating civility, experiencing civility and enacting civility—bears some similarities with Kerr's (1999) conceptualisation of education for citizenship as comprising educating about citizenship, educating through citizenship and educating for citizenship.

expression. From this argument, I suggest that in situations where pupils are not given appropriate opportunities for expressing their voices, and where pupils are not exposed to a wide range of other voices, civility is heavily compromised.

Third, by focusing in this chapter on pupils' democratic education and preparation for democratic citizenship, I understand pupils as citizens today and as future citizens. Democratic education performs a crucial role in providing pupils with opportunities to practise, experience and explore their citizenship as well as to learn core democratic virtues, such as civility. Fourth, I recognise that the arguments that schools *should* play a crucial role in fostering democratic virtues such as civility and that schools currently fulfil this democratic role are not necessarily the same thing. If we take the two educational jurisdictions with which I am most familiar, Australia and England, there are reasons for concern about the extent to which the education systems and many individual schools are fulfilling their democratic aims, including whether they supporting effectively the education of pupils' character. Nevertheless, amidst (and in spite of) a range of barriers put in their way, there are reasons to be hopeful and optimistic. As I seek to highlight at relevant points in this chapter, some schools are already doing a fine job of supporting pupils to develop and express democratic virtues, working with others (families, community groups, third sector organisations, etc.) in order to do so. There is, however, general scope for improvement.

Situating Civility

My main argument in this section is that knowledge and understanding form a necessary part of learning civility, and indeed act as a precursor to pupils experiencing and enacting civility. Knowledge and understanding does not equate solely with factual information. Rather, knowledge and understanding refers to the various intellectual resources—concepts, ideas and vocabulary—pupils require in order to understand the meaning of civility (and, indeed, incivility) and be able to practise civility (Jubilee Centre 2017). Acquiring the sort of knowledge and understanding I have in mind entails that pupils engage with different understandings of civility, and examine the ways that meanings of civility and incivility are situated, and are in turn actually operationalised, within given historical, political and cultural contexts.

The suggestion that pupils in schools should learn *about* civility if they are to practise civility is immediately open to two criticisms. Caricaturing these briefly here will help to clarify my precise position from the outset. The first criticism might run something like this: seeking to ground an education *for* civility in an education *about* civility presupposes a *fixed* definition, with this definition imposed on pupils. The practical result of this position might be that teachers conceive and present civility as a concept already determined, neglecting contextual nuances such as structural inequalities that often, in practice, determine the meanings and (ab)uses of civility. When fixed definitions are enforced little or no room is left for open discussion and debate about what does and should count as civility. A second criticism might take an alternative tack: focusing on the importance of context and suggesting that pupils explore different definitions denies—whether intentionally or unintentionally—the possibility of consensus on and clarity of a universal understanding of civility, rendering the concept relativistic. The practical result of this position might be that teachers conceive and present civility and incivility as culturally determined and/or subjective, with inquiry and exploration not moving beyond pupils clarifying their own views about the meaning of each. Indeed, in their study of how teachers of the International Baccalaureate in Australia and Canada focusing on teachers' moral boundaries when teaching about plural interests and dealing with profane language, Walsh and Casinader (2019, pp. 143–144) report that for most teachers in the study "the boundary of morality was seen to exist in the classroom itself on a person-to-person basis, and in some cases, was not located even at the boundary of the school grounds".

Taking these two potential, if stark, criticisms into account we can see that any meaningful, critical form of educating about civility needs to chart a careful course. Educating about civility must provide pupils with sufficient definitional clarity that they are able to comprehend what civility is and requires of citizens in general terms, and in the proceeding chapters I have offered a way of conceptualising civility that I think offers a viable approach for this purpose. To understand civility, that is, pupils need to consider what civic conduct is needed by citizens (listening to the interests of others and sharing one's own interests, being open-minded, eschewing dogmatism, being open to areas of agreement, being willing to amend one's view on the receipt of new information, etc.), how civility connects to and involves other democratic dispositions, such as engaged tolerance, and the ways that civility is intimately connected to the friendship between citizens characterised by mutual fellow-feeling and well-wishing. In addition, educating about civility must enlighten pupils about key salient features of situations, including their own character, that shape what might be a civil action given the particularities of the situation. In other words, pupils need a common language and vocabulary of civility, but one which is flexible enough to guide them towards the intermediate mean.

Here, Carr's (2006, p. 448) reflection is useful. When Aristotelian inspired virtue theorists "insist that virtuous agents are those who act at the right time, in relation to the right objects, towards the right people, with the right motive and in the right way, they are claiming only that justice or friendship (for example) may be variably expressed in different contexts—not that justice takes on an entirely new meaning in different contexts". Pupils need, then, to understand civility on a general level, but appreciate that context remains a crucial factor in determining what the right time, the right objects, the right people and so on actually are, and they can only understand this if they are provided with sufficient chances and spaces for engaging intellectually with key issues and practical examples of civility and incivility. A crucial step in this process is for pupils to engage in inquiry that enables them to explore different definitions and practical examples of civility and incivility (including justified incivility), asking of them that they actively investigate not only what these concepts comprise, but also how they are shaped, used and manipulated within and across contexts. This active investigation represents a critical engagement through which pupils seek to understand and empathise with the interests of others within their political communities (Peterson 2017; D'Olimpio 2018).

It is only through understanding civility and comprehending how "civility" and "incivility" are actually experienced by various groups in the real world that pupils (and for that matter all citizens) can start to consider questions of how misuses of civility might be challenged and redressed. Knowledge and understanding about civility acts as a precursor to engaging in debates about what might be done differently and how structural inequalities might be challenged (here again the recognition that pupils are citizens of today and not just of the future is pertinent). Let us consider the case of deliberative forms of politics, which I have argued in this book provide major forums for deliberative democracy. One of the intended goals of deliberative democracy, indeed a goal that is necessary for civility, is the avoidance of particular sectional and factional interests dominating (Jacobs et al. 2009). In the real world, it is patently the case that not *all* deliberation in public life attains this lofty standard. Yet, without an understanding of (1) a general conception of civility and (2) applying that conception to take account of contextual factors, pupils (and indeed teachers) will not be in a position to make an informed judgement as to whether particular sectional and factional interests are dominating, whether this domination is arbitrary, and whose interest the domination favours. As Bernard Crick (2000, p. 32) argued persuasively, discussing "how should things be reformed?" before a "realistic knowledge of how things are actually done" is problematic; it is to put the cart before the horse.

The pedagogical work needed of schools and teachers in situating civility inevitably involves engaging in controversial and sensitive issues. As examined in Chap. 1, and as suggested by Thiranagama et al. (2018, p. 157), "claims of civility are always deeply ethical, political, and economic—in the broad sense that they are implicitly or explicitly concerned with the distribution of violence and resources, the ways in which and the degree to which the social fabric is hierarchically organized, and conflicts over the meanings of virtue, obligation, and consequences". I have suggested in the previous paragraph that cultivating civility in schools cannot stand apart from the conflicts over civility (though it remains another question as to what age and to what extent pupils should be introduced to these conflicts). A core element of teaching civility in schools is to construct dialogue around actual existing practices of civility, whether in the immediate context (school, local community) or beyond, including historically. Case studies abound of real-world examples of civility and incivility—including those concerning online forms of democratic communication—and these are ripe for exploring framings of what does and does not count as civil conduct, how citizens are mediating civility in fractious contexts, and how these framings and mediations connect with or severe mutual bonds between citizens. So too, by examining collective social action of the past, such as the civil rights movement, pupils can learn the complexities of how public consciousness was raised and change brought about through concerted civil and justifiably uncivil action (Murphy 2004).

Yet, we know that across a range of contexts schools and teachers often have difficulty in handling controversial and sensitive issues within schools and their classrooms (Oulton et al. 2004; Noddings and Brooks 2017; Chikoko et al. 2011). Some teachers seek to avoid engaging pupils in controversial and sensitive political issues for reasons of concern about what contentious views and issues may be expressed, while others do so for reasons of curriculum overload. Many schools and teachers respond to the challenges of engaging their pupils in discussing controversial and sensitive issues by drawing up, often with pupils themselves, a list of rules for discussion in an effort to ensure civil discussion. Whether to guide classroom discussion generally, circle time, or a community of inquiry such rules typically include taking turns to speak, being silent when others are speaking, listening and responding to others and other similar behaviours. Although they may provide help in clarifying certain behaviours expected of students, basing civic conduct on rules, however, has two notable limitations. First, lists of rules in classrooms tend to be domain specific, meaning that even if pupils conform to them during circle time or whenever there is a classroom discussion, without developing a deeper disposition to be civil such behaviour is unlikely to transfer into other aspects of school life. Second, lists of rules do not in and of themselves connect explicitly with bonds of friendship, mutuality and fellow-felling between citizens that I have argued underpin and reinforce civility. As I have argued above, cultivating civility is not only about civic conduct, but is also about an engaged relationship with others shaped by understanding, attentiveness and a recognition of civic friendship. As Richard Battistoni (1985, p. 159) has argued:

> Only by building in students the affective feeling towards their fellow citizens can the foundation for a democratic political community be established. In fact, as the life of the political community progresses and becomes more complex over time, and as common goals and purposes are needed and sought more often by citizens, the importance of a basic affection between and encouragement among citizens grow. If they are not cultivated in the civic education of the young the affective bonds necessary to the continued success of democratic politics will not develop.

Recognising the importance of basic affection between citizens and the way that civility both grows from and sustains such affection requires that pupils are able to engage with controversial and sensitive issues about civility and to understand that while the meaning of civility is not a settled matter, any meaningful educational approach to civility—as with any democratic virtue—must begin from a general understanding that is then examined against particular instances. In this way, schools and teachers do not impose a fixed meaning of civility on pupils. Nor do they focus on instilling a narrow set of rules of behaviour. Rather, they provide definitional boundaries, the opportunity to examine real-life cases and sufficient intellectual resources to enable pupils to discern and reflect on what civility looks like in particular situations in order that they can then apply this knowledge and understanding in their own lives.

Experiencing Civility

While knowledge and understanding of civility is an essential component of educating civility, knowledge and understanding can only take us so far. If civility is to be formed and expressed, and is to become a deep-grained habit, pupils must have opportunities to practice civility and to reflect on these practices. In line with the position adopted in the previous chapters, it will come as no surprise that I consider opportunities to engage in deliberative forums as a valuable mechanism for practicing civility. While the importance of education for developing deliberative capacities is well noted in the literature (Gutmann and Thompson 1996; Gutmann 1987; Maynor 2003), there is also a great deal of educational literature that now that draws out the educational value of pupils engaging in deliberative processes.

In her seminal book, *Democratic Education*, Amy Gutmann (1987, p. 51) points to the fact that pupils need to practice, form and express capacities such as civility in order to "understand, communicate and negotiate disagreement". Through deliberative practices, pupils are able to learn "the open-minded and deliberative spirit that prefigures the way in which democratic citizens ideally govern themselves… deliberatively rather than dogmatically" (p. 37). Here, Gutmann (1987, p. 51) draws out the centrality of moral character and social connectedness that is needed in deliberative learning:

> People adept at logical reasoning who lack moral character are sophists of the worst sort: they use moral arguments to serve whatever ends they happen to choose for themselves. They do not take morality seriously nor are they able to distinguish between the obvious moral demands and the agonizing dilemmas of life.

Similarly, D'Olimpio (2018, p. 198) writes of communities of inquiry as an example of a pedagogical approach that fosters trust and enables deliberative reflective exploration of the ideas at hand:

> When students and a teacher form a CoI, they are creating a safe space whereby the participants in the dialogue can trust each other to build upon as well as to critically analyse ideas.

These thoughts build on the work of Mathew Lipman and Ann Margaret Sharp who argued that neither the critical thinking nor creative thinking central to communities of inquiry are in and of themselves collaborative endeavours and therefore must be added to by caring thinking (Cam 2014). Lipman (2002, p. 271) defines caring thinking as "to think ethically, affectively, normatively, appreciatively and to actively participate in society with a concern for the common good". Laurance Splitter (2011, p. 497) has argued persuasively that recognising one's self as "one among others" involves three processes: valuing self-worth through one's associations; recognising that others also seek this sort of self-worth and appreciating that "self-appreciation and appreciation for others are interdependent and mutually reinforcing" (Splitter 2011, pp. 497–498; see also, D'Olimpio and Peterson 2018). Developing caring and empathic relationships within and through deliberative forums such as the community of inquiry may also help to counter the wider uncivil trend to see those with different viewpoints as morally inferior (Hannon 2019).

Indeed, without caring relationships between citizens, the "possibility of a just society is non-existent" (Sharp 2014, p. 18). This caring and the mutual recognition involved is a necessary step on the path to the civic friendship so vital for the account of civility I have offered in this book. We must remember too, that if the educational effort needed for caring thinking is to be just, pupils must learn to care about those in society whose interests are most marginalised by current political structures and processes. The hope here is that pupils develop their reflexivity, or what Murphy (2004, p. 87) terms "rhetorical sensitivity", in order that they are able to understand how communication and political discourse are shaped by political power.

Elsewhere I have written at some length about the problems that arise when dialogue in schools about sensitive and controversial issues takes an overly formal and structured approach (Peterson 2009, 2011, 2017; D'Olimpio and Peterson 2018; Sorial and Peterson 2019). Formal debating provides such a case in point, where discussion and interactions are heavily regulated by procedure and in which dialogue is adversarial and competitive, rather than collaborative and consensual. An additional concern is that formal debating and other structured, competitive forms of dialogue run the risk of cultivating and rewarding sharp rhetoric without any requirement that the views expressed are held with any sincerity. When, as often happens in formal school debates, pupils are asked to understand positions contrary to their own by being asked to advocate for such positions, the actual engagement with others whom passionately hold those contrary positions is missing. As Mill (1991, p. 42; emphasis added) famously warned:

> He who knows only his own side of the case, knows little of that. His reasons may be good, and no one may be able to refute the reasons on the opposite side; if he does not so much as know what they are, he has no ground for preferencing either opinion... Nor is it enough, that he should hear the arguments of adversaries from his own teachers, presented as they state them, and accompanied by what they offer as refutations... *He must be able to hear them from persons who actually believe them; who defend them in earnest, and do their very utmost for them.*

Learning is more meaningful when discussion is not constrained by the formality and rigid structure that simply does not appear in all but certain parts of the wider democratic culture. Interestingly here, Murphy (2004, p. 82) cites the views of college students in McMillan and Harriger's study who "perceived the rhetorical skills honed in public-speaking classes to be 'antithetical to effective and egalitarian deliberative practice' (2002, p. 251)".

A number of empirical studies now exist that point to both the processes and outcomes that result from the use of deliberative forums and processes within schools and classrooms (see, for example, McMillan and Harriger 2002; Trickey and Topping 2006; Topping and Trickey 2007a, 2007b; Soter et al. 2008; Millett and Tapper 2012; Hess and McAvoy 2015). In their now seminal study examining different ways of facilitating discussion on political issues in the classroom in the USA, Hess and McAvoy found that, in "Best Practice Discussion", teachers used discussion frequently, facilitated student-to-student dialogue and taught students *how* to discuss (Hess and McAvoy 2015). Effective deliberative pedagogies were found by Hess and McAvoy to be characterised by: flexibility in curriculum and teaching emphasis to allow issues to be explored where relevant and appropriate, intentional planning to provide curricular opportunities for pupils to engage in democratic dialogue, cultivating diversity within and through deliberation and the importance of a supportive whole-school environment.

Hess and McAvoy (2015) explain and illustrate how through their teaching expertise, when providing opportunities for pupils to experience deliberation, good teachers identify and explore ways to make clear disagreement without reducing responses to ad hominem attacks in order to keep the democratic discussion flowing. In doing so, teachers keep a close eye on pupil contributions, using any uncivil responses as an educable opportunity for metacommunication and to discuss why a given response was inappropriate. In their interviews, pupils reported that they had to work at being civil in their deliberative experiences, and identified the importance of practice and reflection for their learning. In surveys and interviews with students in these classes, Hess and McAvoy also found that the pupils were more confident in their ability to discuss controversial sensitive and political issues, had a better understanding of political processes and were more interested in listening to viewpoints that differed from their own.

Of course, in order to tease out the sort of educable opportunities for engaging pupils in metacommunication about what civility and incivility consists of, teachers will need to have some general understanding of what both consist of. This need seems particularly pressing in relation to what constitutes incivility. In a recent report for the UK think-tank, *Policy Exchange*, Trevor Phillips and Hannah Stuart (2018, p. 9) set out a list of "the most prominent manifestations of the incivility that is disfiguring public life" as follows:

1. Misogyny and homophobia
2. Racism and anti-Muslim prejudice
3. Anti-semitism
4. Gross personal invective
5. Ascribing malign motives to opponents
6. Enemies as Nazis
7. Dehumanisation
8. Accusations of treachery/betrayal
9. Denouncing "uncle Toms" and "native informants"
10. Conspiracy theory
11. Hatred of the mainstream press
12. Intimations and/or threats of violence

Schools and teachers will, of course, need to adapt and simplify such a list for it to become a viable teaching tool, but the list acts as a useful stimulus for teachers and pupils to examine what incivility consists of. Interpreting these manifestations within classrooms and schools will require expertise, sensitivity and judgement. Consider, for example, one facet of incivility mentioned at various places in this book that has become increasingly common across a number of contexts—treating others with whom one disagrees as *morally inferior*. Divisions over the election of President Trump in the USA and over Brexit in the UK provide clear exemplifications of this trend, with debates and accusations aiming not just at policies and ideas but at the "sorts of persons" who would adopt a particular stance. Deliberative experiences, such as engaging in a community of inquiry, can provide an important mechanism for pupils to reflect on how, and why, ad hominem attacks undermine civility and how they might be avoided in favour of addressing arguments directly. As suggested in Chap. 2, at a time when children are exploring their own views, clarifying these against other views, traversing the views of their parents, peers and teachers, making mistakes and developing their vocabulary, teaching through civility remains a highly complex and nuanced task, and space needs to be made for pupils to explore their thoughts and emotions about ideas and emotions.

In contrast to being *told* to be civil, by providing opportunities to experience civility through deliberation and reflecting on the contours of civility and incivility, young people learn to appreciate the value and worth of social connectedness and citizenship through their engagement with their peers. They learn, that is, to care, to be attentive and to dedicate themselves to working with others to share ideas and interests in the pursuit of common ground. Through mutual recognition, listening to each other, hearing each other's viewpoints and wishing each other well, a sense of civic community will more likely be fostered (Scorza 2004). Of course, this civic community may well start with the immediate community of the classroom, before extending to the community of the wider school. Crucial here is that pupils reflect on the ways in which the bonds of community connected within their classrooms and schools extend beyond the school gates to wider political communities. This latter task will be challenging, given the abstract aspects of civic friendship. Here, it is instructive to draw on Schwarzenbach's (1996, p. 108) suggestion that we understand the general bonds of civic friendship in the following way: "in the case of civic reproduction such reciprocal 'liking' and 'doing' works via the political process, the constitution, and the public standards of acceptable behavior. Hence, I may personally dislike a fellow citizen of mine and yet remain his civic friend; I will uphold certain public standards by which he must be treated in any given concrete situation". Devoid of this connection to the wider partnerships of civic friendship (i.e. when civility only holds for those in pupils' immediate proximity), educating civility will remain narrowly focused and limited, lacking the glue that binds a community and which, in turn, helps to motivate further civility.

Yet, when we talk about experiencing and practicing civility as vital processes in civility becoming habitual, there is also a need to not neglect the importance of the manners and politeness associated with everyday civility. Throughout this book, I have, whether explicitly or implicitly, rejected the idea that political civility can be equated with the manners and politeness of everyday civility. I have, though, suggested that manners may well be a precondition for political civility in the sense that it would seem illogical to suggest that a person who is rude and impolite could, at the same time, be civil politically speaking. I have spent time in a number of schools that have intentionally developed levels of everyday civility as a platform for cultivating a more engaged and connected form of civility. Starting from core actions of everyday civil conduct such as opening doors for each other, staff welcoming pupils to lessons at the classroom door and communicating (through speech *and* body-language) in respectful ways, these schools have revolutionised the conduct of pupils and staff, creating environments that are safe and caring. Teachers and pupils from these schools remark frequently that making the school a more civil place to be has, in turn, impacted on the sense of commitment and community and there is clear scope for focused empirical research to investigate in schooling environments whether, and if so how, strengthening expressions of everyday civility does indeed impact positively on political civility as both logic and these anecdotal reflections suggest they might.

Enacting Civility

In the previous two sections, the focus has been predominantly on the intentional steps necessary for educating for knowledge and understanding about civility and providing educative opportunities for practicing civility. In this third and final section, I wish to offer some thoughts and reflections about the schooling environment in which these intentional activities occur and which, in turn, will undoubtedly shape their nature and impact. By schooling environment, I mean the wider culture, ethos and relationships experienced by pupils as part of their daily lives in schools and in this section I seek to draw out some thoughts regarding the role that the wider culture of the school can play in enabling civility to be enacted.

Of course, the wider environment of schools cannot be isolated from those in the home, the local community and society as a whole. Just as civility cannot solve all of democracy's discontents, so too the ability of schooling and education to cultivate civility will inevitably be constrained if the wider culture—that of families, local communities, religious communities and wider political institutions and processes—is not supportive. In 2018, a letter to parents from the Dr. John Collier, Head of St. Andrew's Cathedral School in Sydney, challenged directly increases in incivility experienced by the school.[2] He wrote:

> The culture at SACS has always been one of gracious engagement. For a minority of parents, this tone seems to be in decline. I am having to interact with too many parents who have verbally abused, physically threatened or shouted at a staff member... I take it this drift is part of a general decline in civility in society, and needs to be called out. We want to be better than any kind of basic common denominator.

There is a notable sense in which these concerns regarding a crisis of civility in schools are not uncommon. In the summer of 2019, teachers in an English school for pupils aged 3–16 rated outstanding by the inspectorate for schools (OfSTED), Starbank School, in Birmingham, went on strike. Their reason, according to their union the NASUWT? Staff were afraid to come out of their classrooms for fear of

---

[2] https://www.abc.net.au/news/2018-07-02/st-andrews-cathedral-school-principal-warns-of-parent-aggression/9929004

verbal and physical attack and had been provided with panic buttons to call for assistance when needed. According to a member of the Union's executive, "when you go into the school, it looks fantastic but once you get in there it's a different story. It's like feral children, as one member said, they're just running around doing their own thing" (Halliday 2019). In 2017, the Palo Alto teachers' union in California proposed a new civility policy in the hope of addressing levels of incivility among teachers, administrators and parents. In 2007, the Los Altos School District adopted such a policy, seeking to foster greater "mutual respect, civility and orderly conduct among district employees, parents and the public" (Kadvany 2017). Research conducted in English schools by Ravalier and Walsh (2017, p. 129) found that "psychosocial working conditions were at a poor level, with primary teachers in particular exposed to negative parental behaviours, and secondary teachers to poor student behaviour". These researchers also found that "a third of primary school teachers experienced derogatory words or behaviour from parents either online or on school premises at least once a month" (Ratcliffe 2017). A Harris Poll carried out in the USA in 2014 found that "fewer adults believe teachers respect parents or students— and that fewer believe parents and students respect teachers". (Toppo 2014). There are many similar instances and studies that could be cited.

These examples are worrying because they suggest that cultures of incivility around and within school communities, however large or small, are identifiable and are having a negative effect on those involved—teachers, parents, pupils and the wider community. Rather than the school being characterised by mutuality and friendship, cultures of discord, antagonism and "them vs us" have begun to manifest. When these negative conditions start to pervade educational settings such as schools, there is less chance that educational efforts to cultivate civility will succeed. This point holds both for the immediate environment of the school and the wider political culture(s) in individual schools work. As Mander (2014, p. 145) poignantly reflects:

> Unless the teacher is merely the last and explicit voice of a lesson which the pupil has been taught unconsciously all around him or her, there is no realistic chance for educational success. For, to take a simple example, how can an hour's lesson on the importance of democracy hope to succeed if, on the way to school, the child passes an empty polling station?'

First and foremost, then, any call for schools to become institutions in which civility can be enacted must include recognition that prevailing cultures and relationships fundamentally act upon what is possible in and for schools. Furthermore, meaningful partnerships between families and schools are vital if a positive culture of civility is to exist. Empirical studies conducted by the Jubilee Centre for Character and Virtues evidence that communication, respect and trust are crucial for partnerships between schools and families in support of educating character (Arthur et al. 2015, 2017; Harrison et al. 2018).

What else can and are schools doing to be and become places in which civility can be enacted as a matter of habit? In the two sections above, I have suggested that pupils need to learn about civility and that they need to learn through experiencing civility. Beyond this, though very much connected, I see the task for schools and teachers as primarily concerned with creating the ethos and conditions in which civility can occur and flourish in informal and, potentially, unexpected ways. In other words, that "students become involved in a school culture steeped in political talk" (Hess and McAvoy 2015, p. 96). To return to a point made in the previous section, such a culture must include intentional efforts, but must also embrace the fact that deliberative encounters within schools will often occur informally between pupils as they go about their daily lives in schools. Given this, the following point expressed by Murphy (2004, p. 85) appears apt for schooling:

> A rhetorical perspective on civil society illustrates the manner in which citizen deliberation is often less structured than spontaneous and emergent, taking place not exclusively in ideal forums where citizens choose from among a set of predetermined options, but in a variety of arenas which are perhaps not formally recognized.

What has always struck me in speaking with young people in schools in England and Australia is the extent to which—and often unlike their teachers who tend to focus more on formal learning experiences—they reported their questioning and experiences of pressing current issues as occurring in informal contexts, such as their conversations with friends, fellow-pupils and teachers outside of lessons. These experiences are often sparked by some key event—within the school, the local neighbourhood, nationally or internationally—and are engaged with not through structured, idealised deliberation but through evolving discourse. The extent to which schools create the security and spaces to allow these informal interactions is crucial. Indeed, the litmus test of whether a culture of civility exists within a school is not whether pupils, teachers and others are civil in their formal engagements, but whether this civility also occurs in corridors, playgrounds and other informal meeting spaces.

A further feature of school culture required for civility to flourish is that teachers care for pupils, exhibiting and embodying positive relationships. Without a relationship of care and mutual trust between teachers and pupils civility is unlikely to materialise, leading to "a sense of emptiness and meaninglessness on the part of both children and teachers" (Sharp 2014, p. 85). Research conducted by the Jubilee Centre for Character and Virtues reinforces that in schools with a strong approach to character education "positive relationships were understood by teachers to be fundamental to the school's vision and related approaches to character education" (Arthur et al. 2017, p. 20; see also Berkowitz and Bier 2005; Arthur et al. 2006). The necessity of respectful and democratic relationships within schools is also well grounded in the civic education literature (see, for example, Keating et al. 2010; Riddle and Apple 2019). Schools, then, must be and become institutions that work in partnership with families and the wider community to cultivate a positive culture within which civility can flourish.

Conclusion

I would like to start this conclusion by again envisaging a criticism that is likely to be levelled at the arguments made in this chapter. This criticism is that the approach to cultivating civility as a core component of democratic education I have argued for is too conservative and is, as a result, not radical enough in its intention and potential outcomes. What is needed, critics may say, is an education through which structural inequalities can be actively identified and challenged. In other words, that focusing on civility in the ways I have outlined here will simply disguise and reinforce power imbalances in society.

My response to this possible criticism is threefold. First and foremost, I believe I have paid due attention to structural inequalities and the need to be vigilant and reactive where discourses of civility are exclusive and unjustly dominate the interests of certain groups, particularly those who live under disadvantage and marginalisation. Connected as it is to civic friendship, true civility both requires and enables justice. I have suggested in this chapter that educating for civility requires that pupils understand how civility has been, and is, used to deny the voices and interests of marginalised and, in turn, how marginalised groups have turned to justified incivility in order to publicise and challenge their subjugation. Furthermore, I have contended that practicing and reflecting on civil deliberations within schools and classrooms must include a variety of voices and interests—drawing on Hess and McAvoy (2015) such experiences must "cultivate diversity"—in order to be just.

Second, and importantly, I willingly concur that my position is not radical if, that is, radicalism is associated with sweeping social and political change. This is not to concede or accept, however, that the version of civility I have argued for in this book will not be far-reaching. As I understand the concept, civility offers the possibility for groups with different interests to come together through civic conduct and in the spirit of civic friendship. This precisely involves teachers engaging students in the political institutions, conflicts and relationships that give shape to civility in different contexts. As Crick (2000, p. 33) once wrote, giving:

> Children the lowdown on how political institutions work and what political conflicts are about... will encourage ordinary young citizens, their teachers and their politicians to think in terms of common problems to be solved, and to talk about them in common language, not to build up protective walls of mutual incomprehension. It will encourage them to think morally, what should be done; but to think realistically as well as morally; what should be done that is possible, what should be done in the context of other people's opinions of contradictions, difficulties and traditions.

Third, I have pointed out in several places in this book that while I understand civility to be a key civic virtue for democratic life, civility cannot provide a silver bullet to the plethora of issues in contemporary western democracies. Much more than civility is required if structural inequalities and abuses of power are to be challenged and addressed. Nevertheless, and again as I have sought to suggest in the pages of this book, civility can form *part* of the solution by making possible forms of deliberation characterised by an engaged form of tolerance and a commitment to mutual fellow-feeling and well-wishing.

My aim, then, has not been to suggest a revolution, but to suggest a constructive dialogue about civility—its meanings, (ab)uses, practise and so on—within schools and classrooms and to suggest that civility should be a default position for citizens. Subject to further evidence and the conditions for justified incivility set out in Chap. 2, pupils as citizens of today and of the future should learn to conduct themselves civilly and to understand democratic life as a "cooperative activity" (Laden 2019, p. 23). In doing so, they will come to conceive themselves as part of a civic partnership that acts as a basis for, and that gives meaning to, their engagement with others. Of course, in cultures driven by competition, choice and individualisation, the educational task of engendering and sustaining civic partnerships is not without significant challenge. Without civic partnerships, however, it seems unlikely that more healthy forms of cooperative democratic schooling, or for that matter politics, will evolve. Furthermore, while it is important that schools and teachers take an intentional approach towards civility, they must approach the task with flexibility, responding to educative opportunities as they arise in the daily experiences of school life. Through learning about and participating in deliberative encounters, supported by the wider culture of the school and community, pupils will develop their own agency and will come to appreciate the social and democratic importance of civil communication. The hope is that through careful and directed reflection and experiential practice, children will form the habits of civility, being motivated and able to discern and enact the civil response in any given situation.

References

Arthur, J., Deakin Crick, R., Samuel, E., Wilson, K., & McGettrick, B. (2006). *Learning for life. Character education: The formation of virtues and dispositions in 16-19 year olds with particular reference to the religious and spiritual.* Canterbury, CT: Canterbury Christ Church University and University of Bristol.

Arthur, J., Harrison, T., Burn, E., & Moller, F. (2017). *Schools of virtue: Character education in three Birmingham schools.* Birmingham, UK: University of Birmingham.

Arthur, J., Kristjánsson, K., Walker, D., Sanderse, W., Jones, C., Thoma, S., Curren, R., & Roberts, M. (2015). *Character education in UK schools.* Birmingham, UK: University of Birmingham.

Australian Curriculum, Assessment and Reporting Authority. (2018). *The Australian curriculum: Civics and citizenship education.* Retrieved February 20, 2019, from https://www.australian-curriculum.edu.au/f-10-curriculum/humanities-and-social-sciences/civics-and-citizenship/

Battistoni, R. (1985). *Public schooling and the education of democratic citizens.* Jackson, MS: University of Mississippi Press.

Berkowitz, M., & Bier, M. (2005). *What works in character education: A research driven guide for educators.* Retrieved July 24, 2019, from file://adf/css/staff/home/PetersoA/desktop/whatworksinjrce2007.pdf

Cam, P. (2014). 'Commentary on Ann Margaret sharp's "the other dimension of caring thinking". *Journal of Philosophy in Schools, 1*(1), 15.

Carr, D. (2006). The moral roots of citizenship: Reconciling principle and character in citizenship education. *Journal of Moral Education., 35*(4), 443–456.

Chikoko, V., Gilmour, J. D., Harber, C., & Serf, J. (2011). Teaching controversial issues and teacher education in England and South Africa. *Journal of Education for Teaching, 37*(1), 5–19.

Crick, B. (2000). *Essays on citizenship*. London: Continuum.

D'Olimpio, L. (2018). *Media and moral education: A philosophy of critical engagement*. London: Routledge.

D'Olimpio, L., & Peterson, A. (2018). The ethics of narrative art: Philosophy in schools, compassion and learning from stories. *Journal of Philosophy in Schools, 5*(1), 92–110.

Gutmann, A. (1987). *Democratic education*. Princeton, NJ: Princeton University Press.

Gutmann, A., & Thompson, D. (1996). *Democracy and disagreement*. Cambridge, MA: Harvard University Press.

Halliday, J. (2019, June 27). Teachers strike over pupils 'carrying knives and brawling'. *The Guardian Online*. Retrieved July 7, 2019, from https://www.theguardian.com/uk-news/2019/jun/27/teachers-strike-pupils-carrying-knives-brawling-starbank-birmingham

Hannon, M. (2019). Empathetic understanding and deliberative democracy. *Philosophy and Phenomenological Research*. https://doi.org/10.1111/phpr.12624.

Harrison, T., Dineen, K., & Moller, F. (2018). *Parent-teacher partnerships: Barriers and enablers to collaborative character education – Initial insights*. Birmingham, UK: University of Birmingham.

Hess, D., & McAvoy, P. (2015). *The political classroom: Evidence and ethics in democratic education*. New York and London: Routledge.

Jacobs, L. R., Cook, F. L., & Delli Carpini, M. X. (2009). *Talking together: Public deliberation and political participation in America*. Chicago: University of Chicago Press.

Jubilee Centre for Character and Virtues. (2017). *A framework for character education in schools*. Birmingham, UK: University of Birmingham.

Kadvany, E. (2017, October 20). School district considers civility policy. *Palo Alto Online*. Retrieved July 07, 2019, from https://www.paloaltoonline.com/news/2017/10/20/school-district-considers-civility-policy

Keating, A., Kerr, D., Benton, T., Munday, E., & Lopes, J. (2010). *Citizenship education in England 2001–2010: Young people's practices and prospects for the future: The eighth and final report from the citizenship education longitudinal study. Research brief*. London: DfE.

Kerr, D. (1999). Citizenship education in the curriculum: An international review. *The School Field, X*(3/4), 5–32.

Laden, A. S. (2019). Two concepts of civility. In R. G. Boatright, T. J. Shaffer, S. Sobieraj, & D. Goldthwaite Young (Eds.), *A crisis of civility? Political discourse and its discontents* (pp. 9–30). New York: Routledge.

Lipman, M. (2002). *Thinking in education* (2nd ed.). New York: Cambridge University Press.

Mander, W. J. (2014). British idealism and education for citizenship. In T. Brooks (Ed.), *Ethical citizenship: British idealism and the politics of recognition* (pp. 139–158). Basingstoke, UK: Palgrave.

Maynor, J. W. (2003). *Republicanism in the modern world*. Cambridge, MA: Polity Press.

McMillan, J. J., & Harriger, J. (2002). College education and deliberation: A benchmark study. *Communication Education, 51*, 237–253.

Mill, J. S. (1991). *On liberty and other essays*. Oxford: Oxford University Press.

Millett, S., & Tapper, A. (2012). Benefits of collaborative philosophical inquiry in schools. *Educational Philosophy and Theory, 44*(5), 546–567.

Murphy, T. A. (2004). Deliberative civic education and civil society: A consideration of ideals and actualities in democracy and communication education. *Communication Education, 53*(1), 74–91.

Noddings, N., & Brooks, L. (2017). *Teaching controversial issues: The case for critical thinking and moral commitment in the classroom*. New York: Teachers College Press.

Oulton, C., Dillon, J., & Grace, M. (2004). Reconceptualizing the teaching of controversial issues. *International Journal of Social Science Education, 26*(4), 411–423.

Peterson, A. (2009). Civic republicanism and contestatory deliberation: Framing pupil discourse within citizenship education. *British Journal of Educational Studies, 57*(1), 55–69.

Peterson, A. (2011). *Civic republicanism and civic education: The education of citizens.* London: Palgrave.

Peterson, A. (2017). *Compassion and education: Cultivating compassionate children, schools and communities.* Basingstoke, UK: Palgrave.

Phillips, T., & Stuart, H. (2018). *An age of incivility: Understanding the new politics.* London: Policy Exchange.

Qualifications and Curriculum Authority. (2007). *The national curriculum for citizenship* (key stages 3 and 4). London: QCA.

Quigley, C. N., & Buchanan, J. H., Jr. (1991). *Civitas: A framework for civic education.* Calabasas, CA: Center for Civic Education.

Ratcliffe, R. (2017, April 30). Teacher knows best? Not any longer as parents muscle in on the classroom. *The Guardian Online.* Retrieved July 18, 2019, from https://www.theguardian.com/education/2017/apr/29/schools-parents-pupils-education-teachers

Ravalier, J. M., & Walsh, J. (2017). Working conditions and stress in the English education system. *Occupational Medicine, 68,* 129–134.

Riddle, S., & Apple, M. W. (Eds.). (2019). *Re-imagining education for democracy.* New York: Routledge.

Schwarzenbach, S. A. (1996). On civic friendship. *Ethics, 107*(1), 97–128.

Scorza, J. (2004). Liberal citizenship and civic friendship. *Political Theory, 32*(1), 85–108.

Sharp, A. M. (2014). The other dimension of caring thinking. *Journal of Philosophy in Schools, 1*(1), 16–21.

Sorial, S., & Peterson, A. (2019). Australian schools as deliberative spaces: Framing the goal of active and informed citizenship. *The Curriculum Journal, 30*(1), 24–39.

Soter, A. O., Wilkinson, I. A., Murphy, P. K., Rudge, L., Reninger, K., & Edwards, M. (2008). What the discourse tells us: Talk and indicators of high-level comprehension. *International Journal of Educational Research, 47,* 372–391.

Splitter, L. (2011). Identity, citizenship and moral education. *Educational Philosophy and Theory, 43*(5), 484–505.

Thiranagama, S., Kelly, T., & Forment, C. (2018). Introduction: Whose civility? *Anthropological Theory, 18*(2–3), 153–174.

Topping, K., & Trickey, S. (2007a). Collaborative philosophical enquiry for school children: Cognitive effects at 10–12 years. *British Journal of Educational Psychology, 77,* 271–288.

Topping, K., & Trickey, S. (2007b). Collaborative philosophical inquiry for schoolchildren: Cognitive gains at 2-year follow-up. *British Journal of Educational Psychology, 77,* 787–796.

Toppo, G. (2014, January 23) Respect at school in decline, survey shows. *USA Today.* Retrieved July 18, 2019, from https://eu.usatoday.com/story/news/nation/2014/01/23/respect-schools-teachers-parents-students/4789283/

Trickey, S., & Topping, K. (2006). Collaborative philosophical enquiry for school children: Socio-emotional effects at 11-12 years. *School Psychology International, 27*(5), 599–614.

Walsh, L., & Casinader, N. (2019). Investigating the moral territories of international education: A study of the impact of experience, perspectives and dispositions on teachers' engagement with difference in the international baccalaureate primary years Programme. *International Research in Geographical and Environmental Education, 28*(2), 136–150.

Chapter 5
Moving Beyond the "Plight of Civility" and Future Research on Civility and Democratic Education

Abstract In this final, concluding chapter, the key themes and arguments of the book are summarised. Some reflections are also offered about how we might move beyond the "plight of civility" in positive ways and by recognising that cultivating civility involves habits of the mind and heart. The chapter also identifies three research priorities, each with associated research questions, which might usefully guide further theoretical and empirical research about educating civility in schools.

Keywords Research priorities · Civil conduct · Mutual fellow-feeling · "Plight of civility" · Educating civility

My aims in this book have been to examine civility as a civic virtue for democratic life, to offer a conception of civility as comprising civil conduct and mutual fellow-feeling and to explore how schools might educate civility as a core feature of democratic education. In this short concluding chapter, I summarise the key arguments of the book before suggesting some potentially fertile areas for further thinking and empirical research on civility and democratic education.

Levels of civility are a key marker of the democratic health of a political community, and the widespread concerns about the decline in civility and increase in incivility in public life signify this importance of civility for contemporary democratic life. In response to growing concerns about incivility a flurry of commissions, enquires and charters for civility have materialised (see, for example, the Policy Exchange's Civility Hub,[1] the Commission on Civility and Effective Governance,[2]

---

[1] https://policyexchange.org.uk/news/policy-exchange-calls-for-incivility-evidence/

[2] https://www.thepresidency.org/programs/commission-civility-effective-governance

A. Peterson, *Civility and Democratic Education*, SpringerBriefs in Education, https://doi.org/10.1007/978-981-15-1014-4_5

Tucsonans for Civility,[3] National Institute for Civil Discourse[4])—and these offer some hopeful and positive ways to move beyond the "plight of civility" through recognising the importance of civility and challenging incivility. For example, in 2011, the United States Conference of Mayors produced a Civility Accord,[5] stating their commitment to the following principles for civility:

- Respect the right of all Americans to hold different opinions;
- Avoid rhetoric intended to humiliate, de-legitimise or question the patriotism of those whose opinions are different from ours;
- Strive to understand different perspectives;
- Choose words carefully;
- Speak truthfully without accusation, and avoid distortion;
- Speak out against violence, prejudice and incivility in all of their forms, whenever and wherever they occur.

The commitment continues: "We further pledge to exhibit and encourage the kinds of personal qualities that are emblematic of a civil society: gratitude, humility, openness, passion for service to others, propriety, kindness, caring, faith, a sense of duty, and a commitment to doing what is right".

As this Accord attests, at its heart civility is concerned with how citizens interact and live with each other in their political communities. Civility requires of citizens that they conduct themselves well in order to engage with others. Without civil conduct, democratic encounters are likely to be and become fractious and factional, dehumanising those involved and diminishing bonds between citizens. This reminds us that civility is not only about how citizens conduct themselves, but also about what other citizens can reasonably expect of their fellow citizens. Indeed, civility is a key way that citizens enact democracy based on mutual partnership and fellow-feeling. As the Accord also attests, civility is also about character. If we are to have any hope of moving beyond the "plight of civility", educating civility must therefore be attentive to habits of the mind and of the heart.

Following Curzer, civility can be understood as an intermediate mean between two extremes—unfailing civility (the excess) and incivility (the deficiency). While it is both useful and necessary to work with a general definition of civility, we must also understand that what counts as civility in a given situation is dependent on the salient features of that situation, requiring the civil agent to discern what the civil response is for the right reasons, at the right time and to the right amount. This by necessity asks citizens to be vigilant of situations in which certain interests within society—particularly those interests that have suffered persistent prejudice, incivility and marginalisation—are denied a voice in deliberative processes. Citizens need also to be aware that designations of what counts as civil and what is labelled as uncivil are politically motivated and that these designations and labels may aim to

---

[3] https://www.facebook.com/pages/category/Nonprofit-Organization/Tucsonans-for-Civility-163946010318042/

[4] https://nicd.arizona.edu/about

[5] https://www.smgov.net/departments/council/agendas/2011/20111108/s2011110808-A-1.pdf

silence suppressed voices. Political life is, of course, an essentially human endeavour and what seems so concerning about incivility is that it serves, explicitly or implicitly, to dehumanise fellow citizens. Referring to uncivil language and its use to marginalise the "comparatively defenceless", John Stuart Mill (1991, p. 60) once wrote that "the worst offence of this kind which can be committed by a polemic, is to stigmatize those who hold the contrary opinion as bad and immoral men". Dehumanisation and accusations of wickedness are a worrying trend in political discourse today, and serve to break down the good faith so vital to citizens engaging with fellow citizens holding different viewpoints, including those driven by different ideologies. As Hannon (2019, p. 10) contends "once we come to understand the perspectives of people on the other side of the ideological spectrum, we can begin to have a sensible discussion about what divides us". In turn, knowing what divides us provides an important basis from which to seek a mutually acceptable accommodation of difference. The following words from John F. Kennedy's inaugural address on 20th January 1961 remain prescient:

> So let us begin anew--remembering on both sides that civility is not a sign of weakness, and sincerity is always subject to proof. Let us never negotiate out of fear. But let us never fear to negotiate. Let both sides explore what problems unite us instead of belaboring those problems which divide us.[6]

As I also hope to have suggested, civil conduct does not require citizens to be unfailingly civil, nor does it rule out the possibility for justified incivility. Where conditions determine it necessary, incivility may be precisely what the situation justifies. We must be mindful, too, that civility alone cannot address major structural issues and inequalities, it is not a substitute for justice, but may well help to support the cause of justice through enabling the interests of marginalised and disadvantaged groups to be publicised and heard. As Michael Sandel (2010, p. 261) argues:

> A just society can't be achieved simply by maximizing utility or by securing freedom of choice. To achieve a just society we have to reason together about the meaning of the good life and to create a public culture hospitable to the disagreements that will inevitably arise.

This reasoning together is made possible by civility, yet civility offers democracy much more. Writing in the 1970s Michael Walzer (1974, p. 606) posed the following reflection about civility in the liberal state:

> The new citizenship, however, leaves many Americans dissatisfied. Liberalism, even at its most permissive, is a hard politics because it offers so few emotional rewards; the liberal state is not a home for its citizens; it lacks warmth and intimacy.

While not able to deliver the intimacy associated with political life in small, city states, I believe that civility is nonetheless a warm civic virtue, one that bonds citizens to each other as common participants and as partners. Through making possible the sharing of interests and the development of empathy and care, civility engenders mutual fellow-feeling and well-wishing. Frimer and Skitka (2018, p. 846) suggest that a number psychological studies have suggested that people judge others

---

[6] https://www.jfklibrary.org/learn/about-jfk/historic-speeches/inaugural-address

based on two dimensions—"warmth (or nurturance, morality or communion)" and "dominance (or competence agency)" and that "warmth is the primary, and dominance the secondary, dimension of social judgement". Asserting the "Montagu Principle[7]" Frimer and Skitka's study reports that civility increases positive social judgement from others, while incivility damages the perceived warmth of the uncivil actor, suggesting that "incivility comes with large social costs and seldom if ever yields benefits, even when negative partisanship is high" (p. 864). Of course, the cup of civility is never full, but fills and empties over time, subject to the continual impact of communicative encounters and wider political cultures. As Gayer (2018, p. 403) frames it in her study of everyday engagements in Karachi, "civility is episodically revealed and tested through its breaches, be they outward negations of the principle of equality enabling coexistence, or seemingly more innocuous ethnic jokes". Civility asks that citizens are conscious of and are attentive to how their words and actions reveal their civility to others.

Educating for civility is a complex and multifarious enterprise. The institutions, processes and relationships of a democracy play a crucial role in cultivating civility or, indeed, in allowing a culture of incivility to develop. Though not necessarily the primary institution of moral and political formation, schools play a key role in cultivating civility—a role that is shaped by wider cultures and which necessary involves working in partnership with others, most notably with families. Indeed, civility represents a fundamental process and outcome of democratic education. In this book, I have offered a way of thinking about the educational task at hand that is structured around three interconnected educational aims: situating civility, experiencing civility and enacting civility. I hope, also, to have made some broad suggestions about what each of these three aims requires of schools and teachers.

Given the complex and contested nature of civility, there remain several pressing research priorities for democratic education in need of further theoretical and empirical interrogation. Although not suggesting they represent an exhaustive list, the following priorities and associated questions seem particularly important:

Research Priority One: How is civility framed and enacted in schools?

1. Do schools and other educational settings understand civility as a key civic virtue?
2. How is civility operationalised by schools, teachers and other educators, and how is civility connected to related concepts such as tolerance and respect?
3. Do schools differentiate between everyday civility and political civility, and if so what connections are made between the two?

Research Priority Two: How do teachers and other educators understand and approach their role in cultivating civility?

4. Are teachers and other educators confident in educating for civility?
5. If we view schools as micro-political communities, what connections are evident between civility and relational bonds among teachers, pupils and families?

---

[7] Named after Lady Mary Wortley Montagu's assertion that "civility costs nothing and buys everything".

6. How is teachers' work to cultivate civility in schools and other educational settings affected by wider cultures?

Research Priority Three: What teaching and pedagogical processes cultivate civility?

7. Is situating civility a necessary precondition for teaching pupils to experience and enact civility?
8. How do schools and other educational settings provide opportunities for pupils to deliberate with others who hold views different to their own?
9. How do teachers and other educators handle incivility in schools and classrooms and what tools do they use to support this?
10. How are social media offering opportunities for pupils to experience and enact civility and incivility, and through what mechanisms are schools seeking to mediate this?

There are likely to be other research priorities and associated questions that can be added to these ten, but hopefully they provide a good starting point.

To close, I would like to offer the following personal reflection. When I have discussed the fact that I have been working on a book about civility and democratic education with other academics I have received two responses. The first, more positive response, has been to agree that the book is timely and that the need for explorations of civility in education is pressing. The second response has been to express surprise at my decision to advocate for civility. This surprise has been predicated on two not unrelated concerns—first, that civility is merely about politeness and manners and, second, that civility is used too often as a tool to preserve unequal power relations. For both reasons, those academics whom have offered the second response have questioned whether civility can ever be a valuable civic virtue for democratic life. My hope is that in the pages of this book I have offered enough to convince them, and readers more generally, that there is sufficient value in civility to warrant much greater attention in educational literature on civic and character education in democracies today.

References

Frimer, J. A., & Skitka, L. J. (2018). The Montagu principle: Incivility decreases politicians' public approval, even with their political base. *Journal of Personality and Social Psychology: Interpersonal Relations and Group Processes, 115*(5), 845–866.

Gayer, L. (2018). Drawing the line: Bonds and bounds of civility in a Christian *basti* of Karachi. *Anthropological Theory, 18*(2–3), 382–408.

Hannon, M. (2019). Empathetic understanding and deliberative democracy. *Philosophy and Phenomenological Research*. https://doi.org/10.1111/phpr.12624.

Mill, J. S. (1991). *On liberty and other essays*. Oxford, UK: Oxford University Press.

Sandel, M. (2010). *Justice. What's the right thing to do?* London: Penguin.

Walzer, M. (1974). Civility and civic virtue in contemporary America. *Social Research, 41*(4), 593–611.

9 789811 510137